CONTENTS

PREFACE

To the student

Access books are written mainly for students studying for examinations at higher level, particularly GCE Advanced Subsidiary (AS) level and Advanced (A) level. A number of features have been included to assist students, such as the study guides at the end of chapters.

To use these books most effectively, you should be aware of the following features:

- At the beginning of each chapter there is a checklist, which is a brief introduction about the key elements that the chapter covers.
- Key questions, words, people, thoughts and quotes in the margin highlight specific points from the main text.
- Profiles of key individuals give information on a philosopher's background and work.
- There are summary diagrams throughout the chapters to aid revision.
- The revision checklist at the end of each chapter summarises the main points.

General advice on answering essay questions

Structured questions will tell you what to include. The following advice is for those questions which leave it to you to work out.

- The most important thing is to read the question carefully and work out what it really means. Make sure you understand all the words in the question (you may need to check some of them in the dictionary or look up technical terms in the glossary at the back of this book).
- Gather the relevant information for answering the question. You will probably not need everything you know on the topic. Keep to what the question is asking.
- Organise your material by drawing up a plan of paragraphs. Make sure that each paragraph is relevant to the question. Include different views within your answer (most questions require arguments for and against).

- Start with an introduction that explains in your own words what the question is asking and defines any technical words. Work through your answer in carefully planned paragraphs. Write a brief conclusion in which you sum up your answer to the question (without repeating everything in the essay).

1 INTRODUCTION

Chapter checklist

This chapter introduces what is involved in the study of ethics, makes the distinction between descriptive and normative ethics, introduces applied and meta-ethics, and gives a brief historical overview of the history of ethical theory.

Ethics – also known as 'moral philosophy' – is the study of right and wrong, of how people behave, of the moral choices they make and of the ways in which they seek to justify them. Ethics is therefore an enormous subject, covering almost every aspect of life. This book is concerned specifically with ethical theory: with the ways in which people decide whether an action is right or wrong and with the meaning and significance of moral statements. Other books in this series are concerned with applied ethics – with the facts and arguments that relate these theories to actual moral issues – these include *Medical Ethics*, *Issues of Life and Death* and *Social Ethics*.

1 Four basic approaches

In order to make the subject more manageable, we need to start by mapping out different areas of ethics. There are four basic approaches:

a) Descriptive ethics

Key word

Descriptive ethics: descriptions of human moral behaviour.

Descriptive ethics examines the moral choices and values that are held in a particular society. So, for example, one might say that certain societies allow polygamy and others do not, or that some impose the death sentence for certain crimes. Not only can you describe what people do, you can also give an objective description of the reasons they give for doing it. Such descriptive ethics is part sociology and part moral psychology. But the key feature of all descriptive ethics is that it does not examine or question issues of right or wrong. It simply states what is the case.

In itself, descriptive ethics is therefore quite limited, and a student who tried to answer an ethical question simply by describing situations and people's moral decisions would not be considered to have got to grips with the subject. To do that, it is necessary to take the further step of asking whether those decisions were right or wrong, and to examine the reasoning behind the moral decisions people make.

b) Normative ethics

Normative ethics examines the norms, or principles, that people use when they make moral choices. It involves questions about one's *duty* (what one 'ought' to do, often termed **deontological questions**) and questions about the *values* that are expressed through moral choices (sometimes termed **axiological questions**) and what constitutes a 'good' life. Normative ethics takes the step that descriptive ethics avoids. It looks at a statement about behaviour and asks 'Is it right to do that?' So, for example, in descriptive ethics you simply point out the number of abortions that take place. In normative ethics you go on to ask 'But is it *right* to have an abortion?' In other words, you are asking about the norms of behaviour – the bases upon which people decide right from wrong.

c) Meta-ethics

Ethical theory includes discussion of what moral language is all about and how it can be justified. Such discussion is sometimes described as **meta-ethics**. During much of the twentieth century there was a general tendency in Britain and the United States for philosophers to concentrate on language. In other words, instead of simply asking 'Is it right?' they tended to ask 'What does it mean to say that something is right?' or 'What am I doing when I make that sort of statement?' This was in response to a line of thinking that said that all moral propositions were meaningless, since they could not be proved with reference to experienced facts. Meta-ethics represented the attempt to find out what people did mean – since, clearly, those who argued that things were right or wrong thought that what they said definitely *did* have meaning!

d) Applied ethics

The most important and immediate aspect of ethics however is **applied ethics**. There would be no interest in ethics at all unless there were issues where genuine moral choices and values were expressed and questioned. Some of the most important areas of applied ethics today concern the ethics of life and death, medical ethics, the ethics of sexuality and relationships, feminist ethics,

Key thought

Facts alone do not determine whether something is right or wrong.

Key words

Normative ethics: arguments about right and wrong (the 'norms' of behaviour).

Deontological: to do with duty.

Axiological: to do with values.

Key word

Meta-ethics: the examination of the nature of ethical statements.

Key thought

'Is it all nonsense?' If you try to answer that question, you engage in 'meta-ethics'.

Key word

Applied ethics: the application of ethical theory to specific issues.

bioethics (particularly issues concerning genetics), legal ethics, environmental ethics, business ethics and particularly the issues of peace, war and terrorism.

Books on applied ethics examine the choices that are made in these spheres in the light of ethical theories. Ethical theory and applied ethics need to be examined alongside one another. It is not enough to show that a theory is logical, it needs to be tested out by applying it to practical situations to see if it yields reasonable results. Equally, you can reflect on common-sense moral decisions and ask yourself what ethical theories are presupposed by them. So this book offers you half of what you need to appreciate ethical arguments.

2 A historical perspective

Key people

Plato (c428–347BCE)
introduces ideals and the 'form of the good'.

Aristotle (384–322BCE)
introduces the natural law argument, based on a rational view of purpose in the world.

Aquinas (1225–74)
combines Aristotle with Christian beliefs.

Hobbes (1588–1679)
suggests morality is based on agreement, to avoid chaos.

Hume (1711–76)
suggests morality is based on the emotion of good will towards others.

Bentham (1748–1832) and **Mill (1806–73)** develop the theory of utilitarianism.

Kant (1724–1804)
introduces morality based on reason and the idea of duty.

Nietzsche (1844–1900)
challenges Christian morality, and challenges mankind to evolve.

Sartre (1905–80)
claims existential morality encourages you to become fully yourself.

Ethical theory is a branch of philosophy and, as such, has been influenced by the general questions about life and its meaning that have been asked by philosophers over the centuries. It has also been shaped by the social, political and religious culture within which it has developed. To get something of an overview of ethics, let us look at some key features in the history of ethical theory within Western thought:

- In ancient Greece, particularly in the writings of Plato and Aristotle, you have debates about what makes for the good life, about the ideal qualities a person should have and about the relationship between virtue and happiness.
- With the natural law approach of Aquinas, writing in the thirteenth century, you have a medieval attempt to bring together Aristotle's idea that everything should fulfil its natural end or purpose, with the Christian doctrine that all things are created by God, in order to provide a rational underpinning for Christian moral values.
- Later we find four different approaches: Hobbes thought ethics should be based on a contractual agreement between people; Hume thought it should be based on sentiment rather than reason, since people were able to have a natural sympathy for others; the Utilitarians thought it should be based on the expected results of action; and Kant thought that ethical principles could be based on pure practical reason alone.
- Some nineteenth- and twentieth-century thinkers (e.g. Nietzsche and Sartre) have considered ethics in the light of the self-development of individuals, or the personal questions people ask about life and its meaning. They argued that ethics is not something to be discovered, but created and shaped by our own choices.

- For much of the twentieth century ethical theory was dominated by arguments about whether ethical language was meaningless. For some thinkers, ethics was seen as a covert way of expressing one's own preferences or giving commands.
- During the last three decades of the twentieth century and into the twenty-first, in response to a whole range of pressing moral issues, both personal and global, there has been a revival of interest in applied ethics and in questions about the relationship between religion and ethics and the moral implications of living in a multicultural, multi-faith world.

3 The challenge of ethics

In its broadest context, ethics is the study of human conduct. It is about the quest to find what is right and good and the best way to live. Questions about what a person 'ought' to do therefore lead to more fundamental questions about the nature and purpose of human life. But equally, views about life, whether they arise within philosophy or religion, will have an impact on human conduct, and therefore on ethics. So ethics relates very closely to fundamental questions about what is real, what is worthwhile, and what has value.

Key thought

Ethics is about taking a thoughtful and critical interest in the business of living.

It is sometimes argued that if we could all live in a way that is both natural and rational, then justice and happiness would follow. But human nature is seldom ruled only by reason, and in trying to understand what is best, we generally have to consider also what is worst in human nature. It is in contemplating acts of cruelty that we most easily start to perceive what is essential about kindness, in acts of selfishness that we intuit what it would be to act selflessly. But can we go beyond intuition and absolutely *prove* that something is right or wrong?

Key questions

- Can moral questions be decided on the basis of facts, or do they always depend on values and opinions?
- Is there any such thing as goodness, over and above the label 'good' that we give those things of which we approve?
- What would convince me that a statement about human rights or wrongs is final or absolute?
- Is everything simply a matter of personal choice and taste?

There was a time – about the mid-1960s – when it could reasonably be assumed that any quest for an objective definition of 'goodness' or 'virtue' was doomed. Many philosophers considered that moral language merely expressed the desires, intentions or preferences of individuals and posed few challenges. A philosopher might be expected to speak about the nature of moral statements, but was not expected to argue that anything in particular was either right or wrong.

Today, however, ethics has been transformed and dominated by applied ethics. The world set an agenda, and expected those who studied ethics to come up with some guidelines. From international terrorism and global warming to genetic engineering and consumer protection, key issues demanded serious moral consideration.

Ethical positions are not always made explicit, and often confused. Pick up any newspaper and you will find a mixture of facts, values and arguments – along with a fair measure of fantasy and speculation, depending on which paper you choose! The challenge of ethics is to cut through the resulting confusion, to separate out facts, values and arguments, to clarify the grounds upon which comments are made, to examine the beliefs and emotions that are expressed, and to see if the arguments are logically sound.

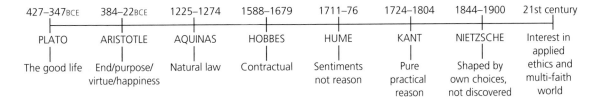

427–347 BCE	384–22 BCE	1225–1274	1588–1679	1711–76	1724–1804	1844–1900	21st century
PLATO	ARISTOTLE	AQUINAS	HOBBES	HUME	KANT	NIETZSCHE	Interest in applied ethics and multi-faith world
The good life	End/purpose/ virtue/happiness	Natural law	Contractual	Sentiments not reason	Pure practical reason	Shaped by own choices, not discovered	

Study guide

Look at the four 'key questions' given in the box on page 4, and jot down your initial views on each of them. As you progress through your study of ethics, revisit them and see if your views have changed.

Chapter checklist ✓

This chapter sets out what you need in order to present a sound ethical argument, the three basic approaches taken to ethics, the issue of how you relate particular situations to general ethical principles, and the social context of ethics in terms of rights and responsibilities.

1 Presenting an ethical argument

You need to be aware of three distinct elements in any good ethical argument: facts, values and the logic of the argument itself. So:

a) You should know the facts about the situation you are considering.

- What does the law say about this situation?
- If you, the presenter of the argument, are religious, or the person whose moral dilemma you are describing is religious, you will want to know what the relevant religion has to say about it.
- You should try to understand exactly what is happening, the motives of those concerned and the predicted outcome of what is being done (if any outcome can be predicted).
- You also need to know if there are any particular circumstances that make this action unique. (Of course, you could argue that every action is unique – after all, no two people are the same. But this means something rather more than that, for there are some situations where someone is in such a special set of circumstances that the normal rules of behaviour that they would follow no longer seem to apply.)

b) You should consider carefully the norms and values by which that action is to be evaluated.

Key thought

There are things you might do if your life depended on it which you would not choose to do otherwise.

Key thought

What may seem a trivial matter to one person may be important to another.

- If you are arguing that something is right or wrong, you must be clear about the grounds upon which you are making that claim, and the values that are implied by it. If not, then you may fail to appreciate why it is that someone else, faced with the same facts, comes to quite a different conclusion about the rights and wrongs of the matter.

c) You should also be aware of the nature of the claim you are making, and of any possible challenge that could be made to that claim.

Key thought

If moral claims are no more than the expression of a personal preference, moral debate becomes impossible.

- In other words, it could be that someone wants to argue that all moral claims are really no more than expressing a personal preference (I say it is right because that is what I want to see happen). If you want to argue against this, you should think carefully about the logical basis upon which you can do so. If you don't, then you will be accused of doing no more than expressing a personal preference, and the argument will have failed.

Key word

Premise: a statement on which another is based in the course of a logical argument.

Like most philosophical arguments, ethical claims move from **premises** to conclusions. The premises will include both the facts of the situation and also the norms of behaviour used by yourself or those involved. The conclusion may be challenged on two grounds:

- That you did not argue logically from the premises to the conclusion. In other words, even given those circumstances, and given those moral values, it does not follow that this or that action is therefore wrong. There might be another way of seeing the whole situation.
- More likely, however, is the challenge that you are wrong about the premises. Thus someone will say 'I disagree with you because I don't think (for example) that you have to preserve human life at all costs, because I feel that the quality of life … etc.' Here the debate is about norms. Equally, however, there could be a straight disagreement about the facts. So, for example, in a court of law there may be considerable debate about whether a person committed some act while the balance of his or her mind was disturbed. If disturbed, that constitutes an important premise to take into account, and the person will not be blamed in the same way as a person who did the same thing while fully aware of his or her actions.

Key thought

The presentation of facts alone does not constitute an ethical argument.

2 Justifying your views

It may be argued that moral language is not really saying anything objective about the external world, but is simply a covert way of

Key word

Non-cognitive: describes a statement that gives no factual information.

expressing one's subjective feelings or recommending a course of action. Such views are termed **non-cognitive**.

On that basis, there is really nothing to discuss. We are not talking about values or principles, nor seeking any objective way of saying whether something is right or wrong; we are simply talking about our own personal wishes.

Naturally enough, a book on ethical theory is going to be concerned particularly with the grounds on which people claim to argue for absolute or universal moral principles, since it is these that they most clearly need to justify (compared with subjective feelings, which require no justification). We shall therefore be looking at arguments to the effect that there are absolute moral principles that can be known by pure reason (*rationalist ethics*) or are commanded by God, others examine virtues and the qualities that make for the good life and what moral positions will promote them (*virtue ethics*), and a third group look at the results of an action and weigh up whether it is good or bad on that basis (*consequentialist ethics*, including *utilitarianism*), and a fourth will ask whether something conforms to a rational interpretation of its natural end or purpose (*natural law*). Others approach ethics from the standpoint of the implied contract that exists between people who live together in a society, part of which may be expressed in terms of laws, and part in terms of the rights and responsibilities that can be expected of members of that society.

Key thought

If I like something, I call it 'good', if I dislike it, I call it 'bad', and there's a non-cognitive end to the matter!

If, as a result of studying ethical theory, you conclude that all moral claims are non-cognitive, that need not stop you stating your moral views. The difference will be that you will not be able to back up those views with reference to any objective facts – about the expected results of an action, or the contractual obligations that a person has to society, or the essential nature of human beings.

3 Theory and practice

This book is specifically about ethical theory. In other words, it looks at the claims that are made about right and wrong, the arguments used and the meaning of the ethical language.

In the course of the book, we shall be looking at a variety of situations. But those who are looking at this book as preparation for an examination course in ethics should be aware that the examples given here are only brought in to illustrate how the theory works. When it comes to examination questions, it will be necessary to have a good working knowledge of the actual situations in which people make moral choices. In other words, if you are looking at medical ethics, it is important to know what the law has to say and what medical options are possible in the situation you are

Key question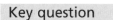

How do you apply general moral principles to individual situations?

considering. Ethics is not limited to facts, but it is based on them. An ethical argument without a factual base is unsatisfactory, because moral decisions are always made in particular situations and under the influence of a number of different factors; leave them out of account and you are hardly going to understand the real moral dilemma involved.

For this reason, there are a range of books in this *Access to Religion and Philosophy* series which give information on particular moral issues. In addition, newspapers are a valuable resource, for they describe a wide range of issues, many of which attract comments about what is right or wrong with little thought as to the norms of conduct which such comments imply, nor the logic by which the conclusions may be drawn from such norms.

a) General arguments and particular situations

When you start to examine the moral choices that people make, you can become bogged down in the whole variety of particular situations. Some of these present clear-cut choices, and the dilemmas involved are straightforward, even if the act of choosing what to do is difficult because the choices are almost equally attractive or disagreeable. In other situations, additional factors come into play and matters are not so easily resolved. *In fact, no two situations are identical, and it is therefore difficult to frame a rule by which all possible situations can be assessed fairly.*

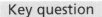

Key question

By what right does any one person say what another 'should' do?

To do ethics, one therefore needs to stand back from the many particular situations and seek the underlying principles that should govern action. But why use 'should' here? You may adopt a set of rules for yourself, but is it fair to impose them on others?

Let us therefore take this step by step:

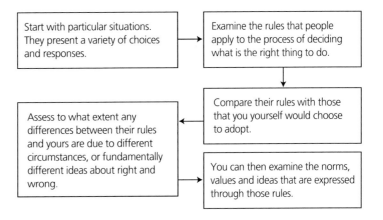

| Start with particular situations. They present a variety of choices and responses. | → | Examine the rules that people apply to the process of deciding what is the right thing to do. |

| Assess to what extent any differences between their rules and yours are due to different circumstances, or fundamentally different ideas about right and wrong. | ← | Compare their rules with those that you yourself would choose to adopt. |

| | → | You can then examine the norms, values and ideas that are expressed through those rules. |

Looking at what people actually do in various situations, and also at the sort of language they use to justify what they do, leads inevitably to questions about the basis of any such justification, the grounds upon which something may be considered right or wrong. In other words, you are asking about *the norms of human behaviour.*

Example

Let us take an entirely hypothetical situation. A president of the United States is accused of having a sexual relationship with a woman other than his wife. He first denies this publicly, but is eventually forced by weight of evidence to admit that he had acted inappropriately, but questions whether what he did should count as having 'sexual relations'.

There are various arguments to be considered:

- Sexual activity between consenting adults should remain a private matter, and should not become the subject of public debate or censure.
- All those who hold high office should accept the moral norms of the society they represent.
- The sex may remain a private matter, but the president should not have lied about it, since truthfulness and integrity are required of someone holding his office.
- Personal matters are irrelevant as long as it does not interfere with a person's job. If the president is still functioning well as president, what does it matter?
- Other presidents in the past have had affairs, so why should this be any different?

As you unpack these and other responses, some fundamental ethical issues emerge:

- The right to individual privacy.
- The moral status of extra-marital sex.
- The value of honesty.

And beneath these there are more general questions about:

- The function of those who hold positions of public responsibility. By accepting such positions, do they thereby set aside their normal right to privacy in all matters that might affect their public role?
- The position of marriage and the family in society.
- The value of absolute honesty as opposed to political expediency.

Key thought

Any historical parallels are simply a matter of 'descriptive' ethics. They do not determine right and wrong.

Key questions

Are we free to choose what to do?

Should each situation be judged individually?

Can the end justify the means?

Does life have any purpose? If so, does that purpose show me what is right or wrong?

Are we just conning ourselves if we think we are making free, moral choices? Are we entirely conditioned by our upbringing?

Although initiated by a discussion of a particular situation, the ethical debate has shifted onto the norms by which that action is judged. Once that happens, it is largely irrelevant to give a list of former presidents who have acted similarly, for when it comes to normative ethics, the fact that other people do the same does not make it either right or wrong.

This example illustrates what we will be concerned with in this book:

- We shall need to look at what makes morality possible. Should we be blamed for things over which we had no control? When is 'I couldn't help it' a valid excuse?
- But once we are satisfied that a free choice can be made in a situation, we have to ask about whether there are any absolute rules that can be applied to this particular case.
- Then there comes the fundamental question about whether there are basic moral principles that should apply simply because we are human beings. Or should moral choices be made on the basis of the expected results of an action?
- We shall then need to ask about the way in which the values that apply to moral choices, and which are therefore used to underpin ethical debate, relate to other fundamental values and beliefs that people hold.
- Finally, we shall have to face various challenges to morality from those who might claim that neither religion nor morality has any factual basis, and that it is all either voluntarily accepted illusion, or else imposed for reasons of social or political control.

b) Every act is global in its implications

Whatever approach you take to ethics – whether based on absolute rules or on the expected results of an action – the implications of moral choice spread outwards until eventually they become global. The issues raised become such that they can be applied in different ways to all situations. It is this flowing to and fro between the individual, the society of which he or she is a part and the nature of life as a whole, that makes ethics so fascinating – for nothing is ultimately insignificant, all reflects a greater whole of which it is but a tiny part.

Ethical arguments do not exist on their own, but are based on beliefs and values that exist prior to the moral dilemma that is being considered – indeed, if there were no beliefs and values, the whole idea of moral choice would become meaningless, because there would be no basis for calling any action good or bad.

It works both ways: ethics is informed by fundamental beliefs and values. But also, fundamental beliefs and values may be left unexamined or unappreciated until being confronted by a moral dilemma highlights their importance.

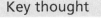
Key thought

If you want to know a person's beliefs and values, look at the ethically significant choices they make.

4 Rights and responsibilities

So far in this chapter, we have been looking at individuals and the theories that link their actions to some overall sense of value or purpose. But that is not the only way in which ethics can be approached. Most moral dilemmas arise within a social context; they are about the way people treat one another, their rights and responsibilities.

It is equally possible therefore to start with society, rather than with the individual, and look at individual actions in the light of what society needs. There has been a long tradition of this, as we shall see, from Plato's arguments about the right relationship between three different classes of people in the state, through Hobbes or Locke in looking at the contractual basis of social behaviour, to thinkers such as Hegel and Marx who see moral norms as arising out of a changing social and political situation. Here ethics overlaps with social and political theories, but its specific contribution lies in an examination of the rights that individuals are deemed to have as members of a society and the responsibilities that such membership entails.

Of course, considering society and its rules raises another problem for ethics: a person may do what is considered 'right', not out of conviction or conscious choice, but only because it is what society expects and as a result of social training. Is such an action genuinely moral? Does its moral validity depend on the individual who performs it, or the society that has developed and inculcated that social norm?

This leads us into a discussion of relativism, which we shall consider in the next section, for different societies may have different ethical norms. There is therefore yet another layer of argument to be added – a layer which considers the rights and responsibilities that actually hold within a society and asks if they can be justified rationally. In other words, is there a deeper reasoning that can assess what society is and how it is formed? This was indeed the concern of thinkers such as Plato, Hobbes, Locke and, in modern times, Rawls. *Ethics is concerned with a sense of justice and the way in which it may be embodied in the contracts – written or otherwise – that bind people together in a social or political unit.*

Key people

Locke (1632–1704)
contributed to the development of democracy.

Hegel (1770–1831)
asserted that every age has its own particular spirit.

Marx (1818–83)
declared that change comes through class conflict.

Key thought

What is accepted as good and right in one society may be outlawed in another.

5 The absolute and the relative

Key word

Objective: used of an argument that is based on external facts or logic.

Some people argue **objectively**. They use logic to reach conclusions from the facts they present. The conclusions reached by such an argument will be true if:

- the facts are correct
- the logic of the argument is sound.

Key word

Subjective: used of an argument that is based on personal views or wishes.

Key quote

'Moral laws are the work of governments or men.'
FINAL WORDS OF THOMAS AIKENHEAD, AN 18-YEAR-OLD STUDENT, BEFORE BEING HUNG IN EDINBURGH ON 8 JANUARY 1697, FOR REJECTING CHRISTIAN DOCTRINE AND DOUBTING THE OBJECTIVITY OF GOOD AND EVIL.

Key quote

'For millennia, most people believed that right was right and wrong was wrong, and that was all there was to it. Now, university lecturers report that their fresh-faced new students take it as obvious that there is no such thing as "the truth" and that morality is relative. In educated circles at least, only the naïve believe in objectivity.'
FROM 'THIS IS WHAT THE CLASH OF CIVILISATIONS IS REALLY ABOUT' BY JULIAN BAGGINI, THE GUARDIAN, 14 APRIL 2007, P.29.

Key quote

'I disapprove of what you say, but I will defend to the death your right to say it.'
VOLTAIRE (ATTRIB.)

Key word

Relativism: the view that there are no universal moral norms.

Other people argue **subjectively**. They present their views and show why they follow from fundamental values that they hold. They may use objective facts in presenting their case; they may use logic to get from their values to their specific moral conclusions; but fundamentally the argument depends upon agreement with the personal views and values expressed. If you do not accept these, you are unlikely to agree with their conclusions.

In fact, most moral issues involve a blending of both objective and subjective elements. The desire to present a moral argument suggests that what is being argued for has broader application than a mere expression of personal preference. In that case, it will need to be presented with some kind of agreed logic, and will also need to be supported by facts. On the other hand, most moral arguments may be reduced to a discussion of fundamental personal views and values. The situation is also coloured by the argument that no amount of factual information is going to be sufficient to decide whether something is right or wrong.

If moral principles are objective, then it should be possible to express them in such a way that you can say that a certain action will be wrong for everyone, not just for the person whose situation you are considering. Indeed, Kant argued that one should be willing for the principle upon which one acts to become a universal law. The more ethics is based on reason and objectivity, the more it tends to claim to offer absolute and universal principles. How does this square with the observed fact that no two situations are ever exactly the same?

a) Social variety and moral relativism

It is quite obvious that circumstances make an enormous difference to what is considered right or wrong. For example, to kill someone you love in order to spare them the pain, discomfort or humiliation of living through the last days of a progressive, incurable and debilitating disease, is quite different from killing a stranger in the course of a robbery. The morality of that action is 'relative' to the situation and the motives of the person concerned.

But there is a more general issue raised by moral **relativism**. It is generally believed today that everyone is entitled to his or her views and the freedom to express them. But observing different social customs and values in different societies leads to moral relativism, since what is right in one society would be wrong in another.

Key thought

The important thing is to understand the fundamental views and values that lie behind different social customs.

Key question

Are values and moral principles *expressed through* particular societies and their laws, or are they *created by* those societies and their laws? The relativist takes a 'created by' approach. The 'expressed through' view may accommodate an absolutist view, i.e. that there is a universal principle but its implementation will be culturally determined.

Key word

Absolutism: the view that it is possible to establish universal moral norms.

Key thought

A relativist will generally hold at least one absolute rule, namely that it is wrong to impose absolute rules.

Key question

What is the difference between 'moral relativism' (the belief that there are no moral absolutes, and that everything depends on particular circumstances) and a more general 'cultural relativism', which simply claims that a person's views and choices are relative to the society in which they live?

Example: polygamy

In a society where there is a shortage of men (e.g. as a result of warfare) and widows receive no social support, it might be considered right for those men who can afford it to take widows as additional wives and care for them. This was the situation in the early days of the Muslim community, for example. Polygamy therefore expresses a fundamental view that women should be cared for and protected.

On the other hand, a view that polygamy is wrong can be taken on exactly the same grounds – namely that men have sexual appetites that outstrip their ability to care for and support the various women whom they might wish to marry. Women are protected by insisting that a man shall have only one wife.

The reason why the same moral value leads to opposite conclusions is down to circumstances. Do we have cultural relativity here or do we have absolutist ethics? The answer is not simple. With respect to the final action that is taken, we have cultural relativity; with respect to the fundamental values and principles we have an absolutist moral principle that it is right to protect those who are vulnerable.

The key difference between moral **absolutism** and a relativist approach is that the latter is prepared to accept that there is in general no way to establish absolute principles and values, but that both value and principle are given from within a social setting.

It is possible to argue that the same basic moral principles may be shared across cultures although expressed differently within each culture. If so, they are likely to be based on those things that are not culturally dependent – on a fundamental understanding of human nature or basic human needs, for example. Most ethical thinkers want to ensure that the autonomy of the individual is respected, and that the norms of behaviour of one culture are not imposed on those who come from a different one.

b) Moral relativism and cultural relativism

To some extent everyone accepts a measure of cultural relativism. It would be nonsense to expect people who are brought up differently to have exactly the same moral sensibilities. From the standpoint of one's own culture, another culture might approve of things that appear to be morally wrong. But that begs the question of whether someone in *that* culture is morally justified in going along with their generally accepted values, or indeed, whether he or she is ever really free to go against them.

A cultural relativist may still hold that there are certain qualities — virtues such as honesty, kindness, loyalty, altruism — that are universal, but argues that they will be displayed in a variety of ways by different people in different cultures.

c) Intrinsic evil

To say that there can be absolute moral judgements, implies that some things are intrinsically good and others intrinsically evil. In other words, that there are values that can be applied to all people at all times and in all places. Thus you could say that the killing of innocent human life is an intrinsic evil. This would be based on a general concept of the value of life. A person guilty of some terrible crime (it might be argued) needs to be killed in order to protect society, either directly or indirectly. Therefore one needs to specify 'innocent'.

Thus, if you can establish that there are certain things that you consider to be intrinsically evil, it follows that there will be absolute moral principles as a result. On the other hand, if you believe that nothing is evil in itself, but only that it is judged to be so by the conventions of a particular society at a particular time, then you will accept only relativist moral arguments.

Alternatively, if you hold that it is always right to allow every society to decide what shall be right or wrong, rather than impose on them an external criterion of morality, it implies that you see the imposition of one person's values on another as an intrinsic evil.

It may even be argued that it is society itself generates evil. Rousseau argued that everyone started life innocent, but became corrupted by society. In other words, if there were no temptations, no sense of the value of money, of status and so on, there would be no envy, no lust for the goods of others, and hence no theft.

Those who argue for absolute moral standards also tend to argue that everyone is responsible for his or her choices. The more relativist thinkers, following Rousseau, tend to argue that bad behaviour can be accounted for by the range of temptations and corrupting influences offered by society, and therefore that society itself is partly to blame.

d) Multiculturalism and the international dimension

Life in the twenty-first century has added an important new dimension to many ethical arguments. Most people now live within multicultural societies. In other words, they will find around them people of different cultural or ethnic backgrounds, and will feel the impact (particularly through the media) of a whole range of values and cultural assumptions.

Key thought

Vegetarians might argue that the killing of innocent animal life is also an intrinsic evil. In this case, it is a principle based on a general concept of the value of all life, animal as well as human.

Key people

Rousseau (1712–78)
a philosopher whose political ideas influenced the French Revolution, but who also had considerable influence on thinking about education and society.

Key question

In a multicultural society, morality will be influenced by a range of values and norms. How do you decide between these? Should there be a common set of values required of all?

A basic question for multiculturalism is whether a society should seek to require (impose, some might say) that everyone within that society subscribe to certain social norms and values. For example, one might ask whether there should be a basic requirement of 'Britishness' for everyone who lives in Britain, irrespective of their religious, cultural or ethnic origins.

In putting together any ethical argument, you should therefore ask yourself whether there are other sets of values (perhaps from a religion) that will influence a person's decision about what is right. You should also take into account the relative strengths of the influences. In other words, you may need to ask whether a person's religion is going to be more important to them than membership of their particular society. If so, it is likely that they will see religious morality as their principal guide for deciding right from wrong.

The other side of the multicultural coin is internationalism. Many issues today have an international dimension, and some – for example, global warming, terrorism, aid to developing nations – are specifically international. In a free market, it is assumed that goods and services should be traded across national borders without restriction – but this leads to the question of 'globalisation', where economic systems and multinational companies are sometimes felt to have a disproportionate effect on the global economy, and therefore on the lives of those who have little opportunity to challenge or question the values of the market that is imposed upon them. This is relevant for the consideration of business ethics.

Key thought

This issue was hotly debated in the months prior to the start of the Iraq war in 2003.

Equally, when it comes to questions of war and peace, it is relevant to ask if such matters should be decided by the individual nations, or whether it is the United Nations that should be responsible for such things.

These are all huge questions and beyond the scope of this present book, but they may need to be taken into account in putting together a moral argument. A thoughtful person, in deciding what is right or wrong, may well want to take into account the global implications in terms of carbon emissions of, for example, what kind of car to drive or what form of public transport to use.

Example

Contraception/family planning may be considered from the standpoint of the two individuals concerned and whether they are willing and able to care for a child. It may also reflect questions about the essential value of human life.

Equally, there may be cultural pressure on them to conform to the norms of the religious or ethnic groups from which they come. But on another level entirely, the issue of contraception can be considered in terms of the global population and the ability of the Earth's resources, or those of individual nations, to cope with their populations.

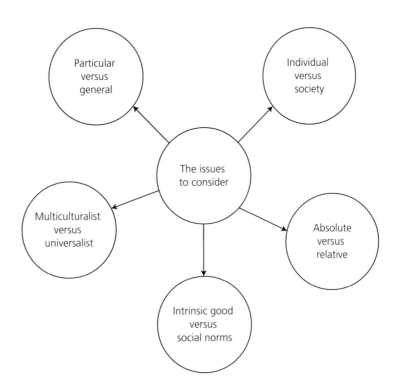

Study guide

By the end of this chapter you should be able to look at a moral argument and point out the degree to which it depends on facts, the principles involved and whether it is therefore possible to say that the argument has universal or more specific validity. You should also be able to take a view on whether ethical statements express only a personal, subjective view or can have objective validity.

Revision checklist ✓

Can you explain ...?

- Why facts alone are not enough to make an ethical argument.
- What it means to say that a statement is non-cognitive.
- The implications for ethical discussion if all moral claims are non-cognitive.

Do you know ...?

- The difference between a relativist view of ethics, and the view that all general moral principles should take into account individual circumstances.
- Why the idea of intrinsic evil counts against a relativist view of ethics.

Give arguments for and against ...

- Both the relativist and the absolutist approach to ethics.

Examples of essay questions

1. The presentation of facts alone does not constitute an ethical argument. Discuss.

AO1

Select and demonstrate clearly relevant knowledge and understanding.

AO1 here would include a clear knowledge of the difference between descriptive and normative ethics, and the fact that ethical arguments are normative.

For AO2, a good response would explain why any moral statement is based on values and principles, and how these need to be set out clearly if the moral claim is to be presented adequately. It would be ideal to give an overall assessment of the place of facts, and whether moral issues depend more on individual situations of universal principles.

AO2

Sustain a critical line of argument and justify a point of view.

2. If morality is based on culture, there can be no universal values. Discuss.

AO1 should explain why morality based on culture does not have universal values. Higher level AO1 might explain the view of morality based on pure reason, in which case there may be universal norms.

AO2 lower level might explore why morality based on culture can have universal values. The cultural relativist view might be argued for, maintaining that they hold certain qualities/virtues that are universal. Higher level AO2 may explore other alternatives, particularly in the context of multicultural issues, and the ethical and political issues connected with the imposition of culture.

Further questions

1 A person who acts in a certain way only because it is what society expects from them, cannot be said to be acting morally. Discuss.

2 Society not individuals is to be blamed for bad behaviour. Discuss.

3 WHAT MAKES MORALITY POSSIBLE?

Chapter checklist

This chapter looks at what is required in order for an action to be considered morally significant. In particular, it examines whether actions and events are wholly determined by their causes, and therefore whether people are actually free to make moral choices. It also clarifies the difference between a factual description of an action and a normative moral statement, and highlights the problem of trying to argue from the one to the other.

1 Three basic requirements

Ethics is concerned with the norms of human behaviour, with the choices people make and the way in which they justify those choices. Therefore it would seem that there must be at least three essential requirements for an action to be considered morally significant:

- that it involves (directly or indirectly) one or more human beings
- that it involves a situation in which rational thought could be applied to the implications of possible courses of action
- that there is a sufficient degree of freedom involved to permit the possibility of alternative courses of action, and thus of the validity of choice.

Let us look briefly at each of these.

a) Human action

A machine that is incapable of thought cannot be blamed for what it does. Thus, although one may claim to 'hate' computers when multiple invoices or some other administrative error is blamed on the operation of a computer system, the computer itself is not to blame for any inconvenience caused. As a machine, it is dependent upon those who program it or use it. If something is wrong, one should blame the conscious agent, not the unconscious tool. Thus, a murderer cannot claim that it was the knife that entered his or her victim, and therefore that the knife was to blame for the subsequent death.

In other words, there needs to be a human agent if we are to apply moral arguments. Animals may hunt and kill one another, volcanoes may erupt and bring about terrible destruction, but none of these things is ethically significant, for no human agency is involved.

b) Rational thought

Generally speaking, unconscious agents do not count morally. That is simply because unconscious agents (like non-human agents) are not in a position to weigh up a situation and choose how to act.

Key question

If 'things' are never to blame, can people be excused responsibility for their actions if they are treated and forced to behave as 'things' rather than as autonomous human agents?

Example

Suppose a person has a heart attack and dies at the wheel of a car, which subsequently veers out of control and kills someone.

The person who has died is no longer able to control the car. The action of swerving off the road and killing the pedestrian is not one in which there is any conscious decision or obvious negligence.

On the other hand, one might ask:

- Did the person driving the car know about the heart condition?
- Had he or she been warned by a doctor not to drive?

If the person had been warned, then he or she must have taken a decision to drive in spite of the dangers. That decision was free and conscious and contributed directly to the death of the pedestrian. The decision, rather than what happened after the heart attack, could therefore be considered morally wrong.

On the other hand, even if the decision to drive had been taken against medical advice, were there exceptional circumstances that justified the risk? For example, was the driver attempting to get a seriously ill person to hospital, being the only person around who could do so? If so, can the risk be justified in the light of the probabilities that could be foreseen at the time of the decision? Could it still be justified in this way, even in the light of the subsequent death?

> Whether justified or not, the moral issue concerns the rational choice, not the events that took place once the person was no longer able to act rationally. In this case, you might blame the driver for his or her decision to drive, rather than for the death of the pedestrian.

c) Freedom

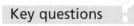

Key questions

Are you ever absolutely free to choose what to do?

If we were completely free from all influences upon us, would we ever be able to *decide* what to do?

Only if you are free to choose what to do can you be held responsible for your actions. A common form of defence offered by one who has been accused of something that is either illegal or deemed immoral is that he or she was not free to choose to do anything else.

You may, for example, find yourself acting as an agent, following the rules laid down by an individual or by society. In this case, you are conscious of what you are doing, but your actions are likely to be considered from a moral point of view only to the extent that you are deemed to be free to accept, reject or challenge the order you are given, or the function you are expected to perform in society. The anticipated consequences of rejecting or challenging that function are taken into consideration in assessing moral significance. Thus, for example, if you obey an order because someone is pointing a gun at your head, the fact that you will be killed if you disobey is a significant factor to be taken into account. Are you free in such circumstances?

In order to answer that question, we need to examine the nature of freedom in more detail.

2 Causes and conditioning

It is generally accepted that all things are brought about by causes that pre-exist them. If this were not so, anything could happen for no reason, and common sense as well as science would be utterly undermined. We may not actually understand why everything in the world is as it is, but we generally accept that (if we had enough relevant information) everything is theoretically capable of being understood.

Fundamental arguments about the nature of causation are beyond the scope of this book, but we should note that there are two ways to approach the matter:

- One can argue that if X is seen to follow Y on a number of occasions, and never to occur without Y first occurring, then we have evidence for a causal connection between X and Y. The more occasions we observe X following Y, the more likely that

Key people

David Hume (1717–76)
A Scottish philosopher, famous for his radical views, his empiricism (i.e. basing all knowledge on sense experience), his criticism of religious claims, and his work as a historian. He argued that moral statements are based on common human feelings of sympathy, rather than objective facts.

Immanuel Kant (1724–1804)
German philosopher who made a 'Copernican revolution' in the theory of knowledge (so called because it was Copernicus who argued that the Earth revolved around the sun and not vice versa), arguing that space, time and causality were features of the way the mind works, rather than being 'out there' in the world that is experienced. Famous also for his distinctive approach to ethics – see below, Chapter 10.

Key words

Determinism: the view that all events are explicable in terms of their causes, and are therefore inevitable.

Reductionism: the view that actions are no more than their underlying physical processes.

Key question

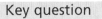

As far as ethics is concerned, the crucial question is this: *Are the causes of an event (either observed or assumed) such that they define the event absolutely?*

causal connection becomes. We can never achieve certainty this way, but only a very high degree of probability. This argument was put forward by David Hume; it is empirical (based on evidence) and it represents the 'inductive' approach of science (see p26). Hume thought that a 'chance' event was simply one about which we did not know all the causal factors.

- One can hold that the human mind works in such a way that it will always seek for causes for each and every event. Even though we cannot find a cause at the moment, we assume that there must be one. This was the approach taken by Immanuel Kant; our minds impose the idea of causality upon our experience.

If causes define events, it follows that everything that will happen in the future is in theory predictable from causes that exist in the present. It is impossible, given the present reality, for the future to be other than absolutely determined. We may think that we are free to choose what to do, but such freedom is merely an illusion created by the very complex process that goes on in the human brain. We think we are choosing, whereas in fact we are running through a very complex calculation whose outcome is already determined.

This approach is called **determinism**, and it is important for the philosophy of science, where is it often argued that Newtonian physics is essentially deterministic. Sometimes the determinist case is linked to an approach called **reductionism**. This is the view that, to understand a complex entity, one should reduce it to the smallest component parts of which it is made. Thus thoughts are in fact *no more than* electrical impulses in the brain; our actions are merely movements occasioned by chemical and electrical activity. If everything is *reduced* to its simplest physical components, and those components can be shown to be determined by the laws of physics, then the complex whole is also thereby determined.

a) Forms of determinism

- **Hard determinism** is as described above, namely that every event is determined by its pre-existing causes. This does not imply that we can know a single 'cause' of every 'effect', but that – taken as a whole – the network of causes and conditions that exist at any one moment is sufficient to determine everything that will happen in the future. A hard determinist would generally take the view that freedom is an illusion, and we are not logically justified in claiming responsibility for our actions, even if we personally feel that we are free and responsible.

- **Soft determinism** is the view that, although events are subject to the influence of a large number of causes and conditions, individuals have their own part to play in the chain of causality. In other words, even if everything is determined, part of what determines it is my own internal process of choosing what to do.

Key thought

Clearly, if reductionism is correct, it makes little sense to say that we are free to choose how to act.

Key people

Gottfried Leibniz (1646–1715)
As a mathematician, Leibniz discovered calculus and invented a calculating machine. As a philosopher, he analysed the nature of substance, arguing that everything is divisible into its smallest possible parts ('monads'). These could not be material, since they had no extension (if they had extension – i.e. dimensions – they could be subdivided yet again), and were therefore to be considered minds (on the assumption that everything is either physical, if extended in space, or mental if not), each acting as programmed by God.

Key question

How can a loving, all-powerful and all-knowing God allow human freedom, knowing that such freedom brings with it the possibility of suffering and evil? (This is the traditional 'problem of evil'.)

Key thought

The more a person becomes aware of his or her conditioning, the more it can be taken into account when evaluating moral choices.

Hence there is scope for an individual to take responsibility for his or her choices – although recognising that the scope for choice will be limited by physical, social or psychological factors. This approach is also known as compatibilism (see below, p25)

● **Theological determinism** – religious believers may argue for this, which is the view (found in some branches of Christianity and in Islam) that God has already determined everything that will happen. In terms of philosophy, this position was taken by Leibniz, who held that everything was ultimately reducible to infinitely small parts called *monads*, having no physical dimensions and therefore mental rather than physical. He believed that God had organised a 'pre-established harmony' such that, at the moment when I would decide to move my arm, for example, the arm would actually be moved by God. Hence, in spite of the experience of freedom and choice, actions were already fixed by God, and harmonised to fit in with my choices.

b) Conditioning

It would be foolish to claim that we are absolutely free, for we need to take into consideration the conditions that influence us and (if you want to use that term) 'determine' what we do. We are influenced by personal, religious, cultural, social and political factors that are all part of our 'conditioning'. Even if we do not consciously reflect upon them, we carry with us values that we pick up from our social environment, either because we wish to continue them, or because we wish consciously to rebel against them. Either way they influence us, and even if any one of them cannot 'determine' what we do, taken together they tend to reduce the scope for free choice.

The awareness of those conditions that prevail at the time when a moral decision is made, is crucial in appreciating its significance. We have already seen that relativism – the view that there are no universal moral rules because everything depends on particular circumstances and particular social norms – is an important feature in ethical debate. Relativism is essentially about whether conditions, since they vary from place to place and time to time, make it impossible to set down universal moral rules.

c) How does all this square with our experience of freedom?

One way out of this problem is not to start with the idea of cause and effect that we find in the world (or impose upon the world) but to start with the actual experience of moral choice. I experience myself as free, and it is that freedom with which I am concerned. It is a view put forward by Kant (see Chapter 10), who argued that we could be at one and the same time *phenomenally* determined (i.e. determined as far as we appear to the senses) and *noumenally* free (free as we are in ourselves).

This is important scientifically, since as our knowledge of human behaviour and particularly brain activity increases it may be possible to predict the response to a situation with great accuracy, even if the subject thought he or she was free – which can lead us into the realm of determinism and reductionism.

Of course, you might want to claim that determinism is false, and that people have genuine freedom to choose what to do. That would clearly endorse rather than diminish the significance of moral choices, and it is termed **libertarianism**. But there is one important point that needs to be established here before we can go on to make any sense of ethics: *Even if determinism and reductionism are true, they are irrelevant to the process of moral decision-making.*

This may sound odd, since if everything is determined, my choice is an illusion and I cannot be blamed for what I do. If determinism is true, ethics would seem to be irrelevant. But that is not in fact the case for, if determinism is true:

- the illusion of freedom is a necessary and determined feature of human experience;
- the experience of choice is necessary and determined;
- the whole argument about ethics is itself already determined.

In other words, we could not, since we are human beings with the brains and faculties we have, do other than get into discussion about ethical issues. And reductionists cannot help but argue that all our actions are reduced to brain activity, because their brain activity determines that they should do so. *If determinism is universally applied, it cannot support one side rather than another in any moral argument.*

Ethics is concerned with the human level of operation. It is indeed true that there is electrical activity in my brain and chemical activity in my muscles corresponding to everything I think and do, but that does not imply that the things I think and do are *the same as* that electrical and chemical activity. It may be that brain activity is a necessary physical component of the process of thought (and the way in which drugs influence thought is an example of the direct link between brains and minds), but it does not follow (as the reductionist claims) that minds are 'nothing but' brain activity, any more than music is 'nothing but' sound waves in the air. Without sound waves, there is no music; but the meaning of 'music' transcends the sound waves that deliver it to our ears.

David Hume was a **compatibilist**. His empirical description of the laws of nature distinguish between laws as *commands* and laws as *descriptions*. The laws of nature are descriptive. They summarise and make general statements based on the empirical evidence that has been gathered – a process which is called **induction**. They do not

Key thought

'I just knew you'd do that!' and 'Typical!' are comments that come as a result of predicting what had, from a person's point of view, been experienced as free choices. They tend to irritate, precisely because being a free agent is so deeply important to our sense of self, and the thought that we are totally predictable suggests that we are no more than automata.

Key word

Libertarianism: those who hold that determinism is false, that people are free to choose how to act, and that they may therefore be held responsible for their actions, may describe themselves as *libertarians*.

Key question

Does determinism stop us having moral dilemmas?

Key word

Compatibilism: those who claim that determinism may be true, and that events may be predictable, but that human beings still have some measure of choice about how they act, may be termed *compatibilists*. In other words, a degree of freedom is logically compatible with determinism. This is also known as *soft determinism*. Compatibilism may also take the form of arguing that determinism is irrelevant to the experience of freedom and moral choice – this is the position expressed in section b) above.

Key words

Incompatibilism: those who hold that determinism is true and is incompatible with the idea of human freedom and moral responsibility, may be called *incompatibilists*, but are more generally described as *hard determinists*.

Induction: the method of arguing from observations to a general principle that offers an explanation of them.

say that something *must* happen, only that it has always been observed to happen. Causality does not entail necessity; we cannot be certain of the future on the basis of observation of the past. Causal connections are made in our minds, as we predict what will happen in any given situation, based on past experience. Hence Hume was able to accept the principle of causality without denying that we have free will.

A detailed survey of the various positions that can be taken on this issue, and of their limitations, is given in Honderich, *How Free are You?* (see Further reading). In particular, it is important to distinguish between those who emphasised freedom in terms of seeing a person's inner motivation as *one of* the causes of an event (e.g. David Hume and G. E. Moore) and those (e.g. Kant) who saw freedom as the ability of someone to originate an entirely new causal series – a freedom based on pure reason, not an option prompted by existing natural wants.

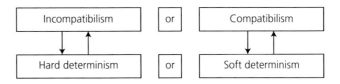

3 How free do I need to be?

Key thought

To make sense of ethics, we need sufficient freedom to act and take responsibility for our actions.

From the previous section we have seen that the experience of freedom is an essential condition for moral choice. We have also seen that the hard determinist argument that we have no freedom whatsoever is irrelevant, because it still leaves us with the fact of the experience of freedom and choice and the need to understand and evaluate such choices. But we also noted that we are all conditioned in some way. There are influences on our decision-making and on the moral rules that prevail in various societies. If we were completely free of all external causes and conditions, we would never stop to think what we 'ought' to do because we would never be influenced by anything that might suggest one course of action rather than another. To make sense of ethics, we need sufficient freedom to act, and take responsibility for our actions, in the context of a finite range of possible courses of action.

There are limitations on my freedom:

- Physical limitations: I cannot be morally required to do something of which I am physically or mentally incapable. (On the other hand, if I choose to put myself into a situation where I am physically incapable – e.g. if drunk or drugged – then I can be considered to be morally responsible for my condition and therefore of whatever happens as a result of it, which would not have happened had I been sober.)

- Legal and social limitations: If the law prevents me from doing something, then I cannot be blamed for not doing it. Of course, this assumes that obeying the law is the right thing to do, which depends upon the nature of the society which has produced that law. Even where there are no specific laws, social conditioning can have the same effect.
- Personal and psychological limitations: A psychotherapist or analyst, observing my present behaviour, thoughts and anxieties, may seek to find their origins in early experience or trauma.
- A religious believer may also claim that his or her actions are directed by God, either by God's having organised circumstances in order to bring about his chosen course of action, or by requiring the believer to obey his commandments.

The above are general limitations on my freedom, but what about those specific limitations where I act under orders? The twentieth century provided a host of examples of political systems which were widely considered to be evil on the grounds of their disregard for individual human rights. Some of those who acted on behalf of such regimes were subsequently accused of crimes against humanity, but argued that they were not guilty because they were simply following orders.

Key thoughts

If a society is judged to be unjust, there may be a moral case to be made for deliberately breaking its laws.

My ability to function as a mature adult may be limited by my past experiences.

Key question

Could a true believer feel that he or she is sufficiently free to oppose God's will?

Example

The killing of unarmed civilians or the humiliation of prisoners of war raises these issues, as does the 'ethnic cleansing' of areas by invading troops. Take the example of a soldier or prison guard who is ordered to 'soften up' a prisoner prior to interrogation. It may be argued that a person has a duty to disobey a command that is obviously wrong, since it involves actions deemed unlawful under international law. In this case there is a conflict of loyalty – with individual conscience and international law on one side and military authority on the other.

The soldier may be physically able to disobey such an order, but may believe that it is in the general interest of ending the conflict that he should obey the command and cause this particular individual to suffer. He may face severe punishment if he disobeys. In such a situation, is the soldier actually free? Is a natural fear of punishment sufficiently strong to justify the claim that he was not free to disobey?

But if that is the case, then what about soldiers in a battle? If a soldier is ordered to attack some enemy position, even though it appears almost certain that he will be killed in the attempt, he is expected to obey that order, and it would generally be regarded as right and honourable for him to do so. Surely, the soldier's action in disobeying an illegal order (e.g. to kill civilians or humiliate prisoners), in spite of the personal consequences, should similarly be counted as right and honourable.

Key thought

A soldier who always stops to consider whether or not it is morally right for him to obey an order is not going to survive long in the armed services.

Does that mean that people under political or military authority have thereby surrendered such a measure of freedom that they can no longer be held responsible for the actions they perform? In this military example, those concerned were conscious, and were in a situation where rational thought and choice could have been made, but they claimed that they were (in effect) merely instruments (although conscious ones), acting on behalf of others. They therefore considered that they could not be held responsible for the actions they carried out, since they were not given sufficient freedom to enable them to be responsible.

a) Internal and external freedom

Key thought

Isaiah Berlin, writing on freedom from a political perspective, made the important distinction between *negative freedom* and *positive freedom*. Negative freedom is about not being restrained by laws (either physical or legal), positive freedom is about the ability to decide what you will do and then to do it.

It is important to distinguish between an internal freedom that a person has and the external restraints imposed on him or her. As we saw above, there are many factors that stop me behaving exactly as I might wish. I know rationally that there would be serious consequences from certain actions and therefore that it cannot be in my best interests to do them. Equally I might value the freedom (e.g. freedom from prison) which I can enjoy if I do not break the law.

Thus, for example, in the UK, I am not free to drive on the right-hand side of a single carriageway road, and I accept that the view of society is that it is wrong to steal. On the other hand, I could *imagine* driving on the wrong side of the road whilst escaping with stolen goods. I have an internal freedom to think about alternatives and decide what I wish to do.

Key quote

'... the only purpose for which power can be rightfully exercised over any member of a civilised community, against his will, is to prevent harm to others. His own good, either physical or moral, is not a sufficient warrant.'

J. S. MILL, *ON LIBERTY* (REFERRED TO AS THE 'HARM PRINCIPLE')

It is these situations which provide the various moral dilemmas, since if everyone automatically wanted what was allowed by external authority, there would be no problem. The problem is that internal freedom allows us to want. Hence I may have a strong inclination to break the law in some way. I feel that I am free to want to do it, even if it is something that I cannot get away with. I may also decide that it would be responsible to curb my freedom for the benefit of society.

Key thought

In the state of Georgia in 2003, a seventeen-year-old male student was given a ten-year prison sentence for having consensual oral sex with a fifteen-year-old girl at a New Year's Eve party, and as recently as 1998 oral sex between husband and wife was punishable by up to twenty years in prison. What would Mill have made of that?

Key thought

I cannot be free to take everything as my own without thereby restricting the freedom of others. Therefore all external freedom is a matter of social compromise.

Key question

If people are not free to choose how to act, should we punish criminals?

There are many external freedoms offered by society, for example, freedom of speech, or of religious beliefs and practices, freedom from arbitrary arrest, or the freedom of equal treatment under the law. These can be laid down by legislation. Other freedoms simply express the possible freedom of the individual to operate within society. Thus there is the freedom offered by education or freedom from poverty, or the economic freedom to work and accumulate wealth. A 'free' society is one that claims to offer as much personal autonomy as possible. On the other hand, all societies place restrictions on external freedoms, otherwise they could not function.

b) Inner freedom and responsibility

The term 'responsible' is used in two ways. You can be said to be responsible for something if you are the person who did it. Daubing graffiti on a police station may be something for which you are held responsible. That is not the same as saying that, in doing so, you were acting responsibly. In this second use of the word, you are 'responsible' when you are old enough to understand the meaning of freedom and law, and you are able to control your behaviour. To be responsible (in this second sense) is not the same thing as being obedient. You may come to the conclusion that a law needs to be changed, and that the only way of bringing that to people's attention is to break the law. In such a case, being morally responsible requires disobedience.

Moral 'responsibility' in the first sense of the word means:

- that you are the person who did something
- that you were conscious at the time (or had consciously chosen to render yourself unconscious)
- that you could have acted differently but chose not to do so.

In the second sense, 'responsibility' requires:

- the acceptance of free will
- the acceptance of rational norms
- the balance of individual, social and universal moral criteria.

In other words, to claim that you are acting responsibly requires you to take 'responsibility' for what you are doing; you cannot claim, at one and the same time, to be morally responsible and also incapable of making a free choice. Nor can you claim to be responsible if you cannot, at least in theory, give a justification for your actions. To say 'I just felt like it' is not a moral justification. Equally, moral responsibility implies that you can weigh up the values by which you choose to live and can assess the extent to which these conform to both the immediate social and legal rules and the wider demands of universal moral norms.

If your foot slips when parking your car, are you responsible for any damage done?

c) The concept 'freedom'

Key thought

Those studying Hinduism or Buddhism may want to consider the role of *karma*, in the discussion of moral freedom. Every action generates karma, either good or bad, which in turn influences for good or ill the context for future actions and choices. Since it is argued that the effects of earlier karma can be overcome by moral actions in the present, karma cannot be said to determine present action (otherwise there would be no way of improving one's situation), merely to provide the context in which present choices are made (i.e. it is 'compatibilist').

In his book *Living Philosophy*, Ray Billington sets out the problems associated with considering 'freedom' as a concept. It is sometimes assumed that there is something called 'freedom' out there which can be discussed and which might or might not exist – as when we discuss the relationship between causality and personal freedom. He suggests quite simply that there would be no 'problem' of freedom if people were not free! It is because we experience and know what freedom is that we feel we have a problem; hence Billington takes the view that arguments about the existence of moral freedom are pointless, since everyone knows what it is to be free.

This view is an important one, since it shows that issues of determinism and reductionism are as meaningless in a world where everyone experiences freedom as discussions about the possibility of sight would be (to use his own example) in a world in which nobody was blind. Hence the danger of taking 'freedom' to be a concept and then debating whether or not it exists.

4 Is and ought

Key word

Naturalistic fallacy: trying to argue from an 'is' to an 'ought'.

We shall see later that the philosopher David Hume complained that many people started to describe what 'is' and then slipped into speaking about what 'ought' to be done, without explaining why they had done so. This point was the basis of a major criticism of ethical theories made by G. E. Moore in *Principia Ethica*, 1903, one of the most influential books on ethics in modern times. He called the attempt to derive an 'ought' from an 'is' the **naturalistic fallacy.**

The general point here is that 'is' describes the facts of a situation. Those facts are generally regarded as morally neutral. They only become part of moral debate when, in response to them, someone says what 'ought' to be done.

Thus, for example, that children are starving as a result of famine is in itself morally neutral. It simply describes the condition of those who die for lack of food. It only becomes a matter of moral debate once, in response to this, it can be shown that a person is able to rectify the situation but has chosen not to do so. Therefore: 'Children are starving' may lead someone to say: 'You ought to do something to help them.' But the second does not follow logically from the first. There has to be a further stage, in the form of a **maxim** (or moral principle) which comes into play. In this case the maxim would be: 'Where there is suffering that can be relieved, it should be relieved.' Once that is inserted, the second of the statements is seen as a consequence of the first. But that maxim cannot simply be proved with reference to facts. It is an interpretation and evaluation of the facts.

In other words: ethics is largely concerned with those maxims, laws or agreements that enable 'ought' statements to be made in response to 'is' statements.

In terms of presenting an ethical argument, one must therefore be on guard against presenting it simply in terms of what 'is' the case. Descriptions of situations, however horrific, do not in themselves count as an argument for a moral point of view. For the argument to be ethical, it has to contain (or hint at, or imply) statements about the principles upon which the moral judgement is being made. Without such principles, there is no justification of subsequent 'ought' statements, and where conclusions differ, it is important to go back and check the principles upon which they are based, as well as the facts they address.

Key word

Maxim: the moral principle governing an action.

Key thought

In examining any moral argument, check:

- the facts that are to be considered
- the principles upon which the moral argument is to be based
- the application of those principles to this particular situation.

If any of those three is missing, the argument will not be sound.

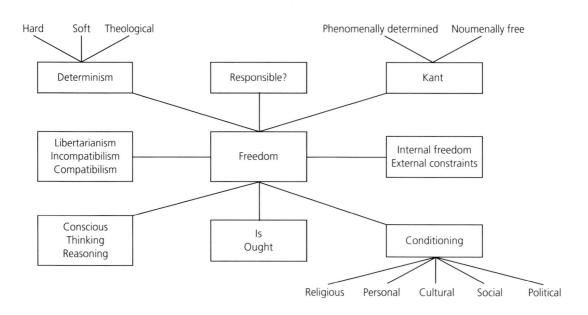

Study guide

By the end of this chapter, you should have thought through the issue of freedom and determinism and come to a view of whether people are sufficiently free to take moral decisions and be responsible for their actions.

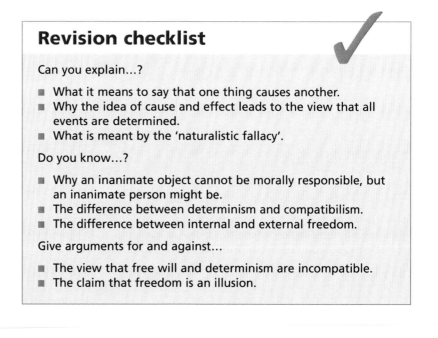

Revision checklist

Can you explain...?

- What it means to say that one thing causes another.
- Why the idea of cause and effect leads to the view that all events are determined.
- What is meant by the 'naturalistic fallacy'.

Do you know...?

- Why an inanimate object cannot be morally responsible, but an inanimate person might be.
- The difference between determinism and compatibilism.
- The difference between internal and external freedom.

Give arguments for and against...

- The view that free will and determinism are incompatible.
- The claim that freedom is an illusion.

Examples of essay questions

1. The more we know another person, the better we can predict how he or she will react in any given situation. Does such knowledge suggest that, if everything were known about a person, his or her experience of freedom would be an illusion?

AO1 here would require a knowledge of the principles of cause and effect, argued either on the basis of induction (as Hume) or imposed by the mind (as Kant). Higher level AO1 might show some awareness of the difference between observed freedom and the experience of freedom.

AO2 would require a student to argue whether the experience of freedom could be considered illusory, on the basis of what has been said about causation. Higher level AO2 might discuss what is meant by 'illusion' and give arguments both for and against the view that the experience of freedom would be an illusion.

2. Explain with examples why one should not try to derive an 'ought' from an 'is' (the naturalistic fallacy). What is needed in order to justify statements about what one 'ought' to do?

AO1 here requires a straightforward explanation of the distinction between moral and factual statements. Higher level AO1 would include examples. It might also perhaps bring in the distinction between descriptive and normative ethics, and why they should not be simply equated with one another.

AO2 is looking for an appreciation of the way in which moral values, principles or maxims are needed to underpin any normative ethical claim.

Further questions

1 Is morality possible if determinism is true? Discuss.

2 There is no difference in reality between compatibilism and determinism. Discuss.

Chapter checklist ✓

Before examining moral arguments, it is important to clarify some of the basic terms that are used. So, in this chapter, we shall look in general at some of the key words used in ethics, and we will then examine the claim that all moral language is meaningless, and some of the ways in which philosophers have tried to justify its use. This study of the nature of ethical statements (as opposed to the study of particular arguments or moral claims) is termed *meta-ethics*.

Should we start by defining what we mean by 'good'? The problem with this approach is that the definition may depend on the argument in which it is used. So, for example, if you are looking at an argument that says that goodness and right action are based on 'X', then the meaning of 'good' will depend on what that 'X' is. If you try to define 'good' before looking at the argument, then you have pre-judged its conclusion!

1 Some ethical terms

a) Ethics and morals

Key word

Meta-ethics: the study of the nature of ethical statements.

Although these two words are derived from the Greek and Latin terms of the same concept, a distinction is sometimes made between them. For example, it is sometimes said that ethics is to do with theory and morals with practice, or that ethics is concerned with general issues and morality with specific cases.

Some might claim that ethics is the accepted set of norms of behaviour for a particular society or group, whereas morality refers to choices that are based on values imposed from outside the social group, chiefly from religious or philosophical beliefs. This distinction is not generally helpful, since any set of values or principles of conduct that are accepted as the ethic of a group or profession, must ultimately rest on fundamental beliefs about the nature of life. In other words, your 'ethic' (in the narrow sense of that word), if it is not just an arbitrary acceptance of a set of rules, must ultimately be based on a sense of right and wrong and on the values that give rise to such a sense. And this, of course, is what morality is about, whether or not its arguments are associated with religious concepts or come about by agreement between individuals in society.

Another distinction is sometimes made, namely that your morals are shown in what you do and your ethics are the rational justification you give for what you do. This is implied by the term 'moral philosophy', which is interchangeable with 'ethics'. Ethics is the rational examination of morals. But that does not mean that morality and ethics can be separated from one another. An action which is unconscious, or in which the agent has no free choice, is not generally considered to be morally significant. Morality is concerned with action that is the result of choice, and which is therefore open to justification, praise or blame.

In this book, the terms 'moral' and 'ethical' will equally be used for arguments concerning right and wrong, the norms of activity that result from such arguments, and the actions that display or go counter to such norms. On the other hand, if a distinction is to be made between the two terms in this book, it is that 'ethics' is used *to describe the rational and systematic examination of moral issues.*

It is also important to distinguish between three terms:

- **Moral** To behave morally is to conform to a set of ethical norms, whether these are personal, religious or established by a group or profession.
- **Immoral** To be immoral is to go against a professed set of norms. Notice, however, that an action may be immoral according to one set of norms and moral according to another. For example, a person who is starving may steal in order to feed herself and her family. On one level it can be argued that theft is wrong. But it could equally be argued that there is a prior moral requirement to save life, and that the institution of private property should come second to this – and therefore that it is right to steal if that is the only means of saving life.
- **Amoral** An action is amoral, with respect to the person who performs it, if it is done without reference to any moral perspective, or to any values that could give rise to a moral perspective. For example, a cat playing with a terrified mouse prior to killing it is acting amorally, simply because a cat has no sense of right or wrong. The same could be claimed for a

Key thought

Distinguishing the term 'ethics' from 'morals' may be an attempt to get away from a narrow sense of morality, associated particularly in Western minds with religious sanctions concerning sexual activity; the term 'immorality' still has that connotation.

Key words

Moral: behaviour that conforms to an accepted set of norms.

Immoral: behaviour that goes against an accepted set of norms.

Amoral: action that is not seen as morally significant by the person performing it.

human who is suffering from a mental condition such that he or she is incapable of understanding the meaning of right and wrong, or incapable of experiencing the emotions that would normally be associated with – for example – inflicting pain on others.

b) Good and bad/right and wrong

The most basic word in ethics is also the most difficult to define. Indeed, it is because it is so difficult to define the meaning of 'good' that we have so many problems in ethics.

A dictionary definition of 'good' (e.g. in *The Concise Oxford Dictionary*) may start with 'having the right qualities, satisfactory, adequate', but it will then go on to give a very large number of contextual meanings – 'good works', 'good will', 'good time' etc. – in order to show the scope of its use. The need to give all those different contexts shows just how varied the meaning can be. The same dictionary defines 'bad' as 'worthless', 'inferior, deficient', 'of poor quality', 'incorrect, not valid; counterfeit or debased', 'unpleasant' and so on, each related to a particular context.

This great variety of uses of the terms 'good' and 'bad' raises some fundamental questions for ethics:

- Is 'goodness' something that exists in things independently of our deciding that they are good? In other words: is goodness an inherent quality?
- Or is it something that we determine by an act of will? Do I call something good simply because I approve of it? Is its goodness related to its usefulness to me?
- Is goodness in any sense absolute, or does it depend on each person's view?
- If goodness is related to our perception, rather than being an inherent quality, do we have any means of deciding the issue when one person calls something 'good' and another calls it 'bad'?
- What have a good knife and a good opera singer in common? What is it that enables them both to be termed 'good'?

As a starting point, perhaps, one could think about the approach taken by the Greek philosopher Aristotle. He saw goodness in terms of each thing fulfilling the purpose for which it had been designed. Thus a good knife is a knife that cuts well. So what is a good human being? Clearly, in order to know the answer to that, you have to understand what a human being is designed to do or be. This led to the natural law approach to ethics, which we shall examine later.

Key thought

We all have some sense of what 'good' means, but that meaning is extremely difficult to specify accurately.

Key thought

These are questions that will need to be explored further in terms of the various ethical theories. And, of course, we cannot get far with definitions of 'right' and 'wrong' unless we first know what we mean by 'good'.

Key people

Aristotle (384–322BCE) was a hugely influential Greek thinker. He considered everything to have an essence, which was shown by a rational interpretation of its purpose or end. To fulfil one's essence is what defines one's 'good'. He considered that people rightly aimed to achieve happiness, in the sense of living well and thereby fulfilling their essence. (See also below, p.53)

Key words

Deontological: based on duty or obligation.

Teleological: based on expected results.

Ethical naturalism: the view that goodness is something that exists, such that you can explain it in terms of other things, e.g. the purpose of something, or some other feature of human life. Examples of this include the work of Aristotle (see Chapter 6), and the Natural Law approach (see Chapter 7).

Ethical non-naturalism: the view that goodness is not inherent in the world, but is a term we use to describe an object or action. Hence ethical statements cannot be reduced to non-ethical ones.

On the other hand it is possible to give some external justification for calling something good. Thus, for example, a religious person might say that 'good' is whatever God commands.

A useful distinction is made between **deontological** and **teleological** approaches. If you consider the rules that govern human activity, with issues of right and wrong, then you are taking a *deontological* approach – in other words, an approach based on a sense of 'duty'. If you think instead about the chosen goal that is sought in an action, or the 'good' at which life aims, then you are taking a *teleological* approach – in other words, one based on the expected 'end'.

It is clear, therefore, that in ethics you cannot simply define your terms and then expound ethical theories by straightforward, logical deduction. Every theory or approach to ethics will, by its very nature, redefine the meaning of the fundamental terms it uses. The words make sense in the context of a theory or overall view of life. Once removed from that context, they become vague and almost impossible to define. But before we look at the theories that explore what is good and right, there is a prior question to be examined: Do moral statements make sense at all? What are they actually doing?

We will examine these questions now in terms of theories of moral language that were developed in the twentieth century, in response to the challenge that moral language is not factual and is therefore meaningless.

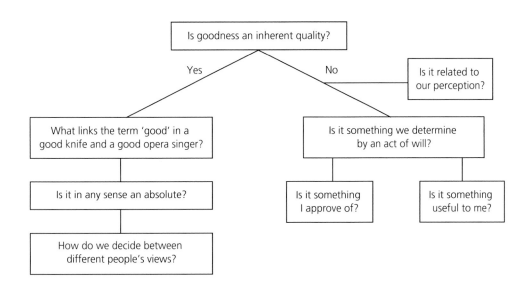

2 Can moral claims be justified?

Key words

Logical positivism: the view that for language to be meaningful it must be verifiable by sense experience.

Ethical non-cognitivism: the view that moral statements do not give any form of information, but are merely the expression of the views or wishes of the person who makes them. This is the view taken by logical positivism, and it is reflected in both the emotivist and prescriptivist accounts of moral statements.

Key people

Ludwig Wittgenstein (1889–1951)
Originally interested in engineering, mathematics and logic, Wittgenstein became hugely influential through his work on language. His early *Tractatus* saw the meaning of a statement primarily in terms of its reference to the experienced world. Later he broadened his approach, with the meaning of language seen in terms of its use.

A. J. Ayer (1910–89)
Influenced by the Vienna Circle, Alfred Ayer published *Language, Truth and Logic* at the age of 26, establishing himself as a radical thinker, attacking more conventional religious and moral theories found in Oxford. He took an 'emotivist' view that moral statements expressed the feelings of the person making them, rather than any objective truth.

Key words

Metaphysical ethics: theories relating ethics to an overall view of the universe.

Intuitionism: the theory that 'good' can be recognised but not defined.

a) Logical positivism

Much of twentieth-century ethics has been bound up with meta-ethical questions – in other words, with questions about the meaning and justification of ethical language itself, rather than with matters of what is actually right or wrong.

The main reason for this was the development of **logical positivism**, a view of language which limited its meaning to that which could be verified by sense experience. In other words, if I make a statement, it is either true or false depending on whether someone could in principle go and check the facts to which I refer. If there is no possible evidence that can be given either for or against that statement being true, then it is meaningless. This approach was summed up as: *The meaning of a statement is its method of verification.* In other words, to say 'X exists' means 'If you go and look, you will see X.'

This view of language is found in the early work of Wittgenstein. His *Tractatus* (1921) was an immensely influential book, which inspired the work of a group of philosophers known as the Vienna Circle, and it was there that logical positivism developed. Its influence was spread by the publication in 1936 of *Language, Truth and Logic* by A. J. Ayer. Ayer claimed that there were only two kinds of propositions:

- truths known by definition (e.g. mathematics and logic)
- truths known through sense experience (i.e. proved by external facts).

Where do moral statements come in such a scheme? If they are known by definition then they are mere tautologies, claiming nothing. On the other hand, how can you point to facts that prove a moral statement? That, too, is impossible; as we saw above, you cannot derive an 'ought' from an 'is'. Hence, Ayer saw all moral statements as meaningless.

This challenge dominated ethics from the 1930s until the 1960s, and we shall examine a number of attempts that were made to find a meaning for ethical statements that would not be dismissed by Ayer's argument. But in order to appreciate the impact of positivism, it is useful to look at two approaches to ethics that preceded it: **metaphysical ethics** and **intuitionism**.

b) Metaphysical ethics

'Metaphysical ethics' wanted to show that morality could be related to an overall view of the world and the place of humankind within it. F. H. Bradley, in *Ethical Studies* (1876) argued that the supreme

Key quote

'The world is all that is the case.'
WITTGENSTEIN, *TRACTATUS*

Key people

G. E. Moore (1873–1958)
A Cambridge philosopher, he was
particularly known for his defence
of ethical statements and his
refusal to accept that they could
be reduced to statements of fact,
as set out in *Principia Ethica*
(1903). Later he was known for
his 'common sense' approach to
our familiar beliefs about the
world, defending them in the face
of sceptical questioning about
whether ordinary things exist. He
claimed to be more baffled by
things said about the world by
philosophers than by the world
itself. His own approach was to
analyse ordinary propositions in
terms of the 'sense-data' on which
they were based, and he struggled
to show how such sense-data
related to external objects.

good for humankind was self-realisation. In other words, we act in a
way that is morally good when we do those things that allow us to
develop ourselves as part of a wider community. Morality is
therefore not just about particular actions, but about the character of
the people who perform them, and the understanding they have of
their part in the wider world.

Now, metaphysical ethics of this sort depends on two abstract
ideas: the world as a whole, and self-realisation. Neither of these can
be reduced to the sort of evidence that the logical positivists were
later to claim as necessary for meaning. Thus, they would have seen
metaphysical ethics as meaningless.

c) The primacy of 'good' and intuitionism

G. E. Moore argued in *Principia Ethica* (1903) that the primary term
'good' could not be defined in terms of other things, and did so in
the context of claiming that most earlier ethical theories had fallen
into the **naturalistic fallacy** of trying to derive an 'ought' from an
'is' (see above page 30). He came to the conclusion that goodness
was not a natural property – you could not equate it with anything
else, or give a description of it in terms of other things. You may
know what 'good' is, but you cannot define it. Fundamental moral
principles are therefore known by intuition. They cannot be proved
to be true or false, but are recognised as soon as they are thought
about. Thus we know what it means to say that something is 'good',
even to say that many different things are good, although we cannot
point to any particular quality that makes it so. The analogy Moore
used was with colour. *We know what 'yellow' is, and can recognise it
wherever we see it, but we cannot actually define yellow. In the same way,
we know what 'good' means, but cannot define it.*

Key questions

Starting from the indefinable 'good', Moore's book raises two basic questions:

- What things should exist for their own sake? His answer: those that we call intrinsically good.
- What actions ought we to perform? His answer: those that produce most good.

Now, in contrast to metaphysical ethics, this approach does not
depend on any abstract concepts about the world as a whole. On
the other hand, 'good' is not simply a word we choose to apply to
objects, but is the name of a quality that inheres in things. He
thought of good as something rather like 'beautiful' – a quality that
could be found in things but not described.

Key thought

Intuitionism in ethics is often used as a theory for how moral claims may be *justified*. In other words, if I intuit what is 'good' and base my morality on that, I do not need to explain it further.

In philosophy, intuitionism is a theory that applies also to mathematics: that we know mathematical principles *a priori*, rather than through experience – a tradition that goes back to Kant and even to Plato.

This general approach – that the good can be known but not defined – may be called *intuitionism*, although that was not a term that Moore himself used for it. His theory was mainly focused on the primacy of the word 'good', whereas a broad intuitionist approach would see all moral claims as justified by intuition.

In a further development of this approach, H. A. Prichard (1871–1947) argued that you could not reduce moral obligation to anything else. Like Moore's 'good' it was something known directly by intuition. (His work on this, *Moral Obligation*, was published in 1949.)

Another Oxford philosopher influenced by Moore, W. D. Ross (1877–1971), argued in *The Right and the Good* (1930) and *The Foundations of Ethics* (1939) that Moore was right to deny that you could equate goodness with any natural property (the naturalistic fallacy – no 'ought' from an 'is'), but that he was wrong in arguing that the only criterion for moral obligation was to maximise the good. Rather, he pointed out that one may have a conflict of duties, and it may not be at all obvious which is to take priority. My duty is therefore self-evident (known through intuition) provided that it does not conflict with another self-evident duty.

Notice what is implied by the intuitionist approach: you cannot use any factual evidence to show that something is good or that one has a moral obligation. All basic moral judgements are self-evident.

d) Meaningless?

Key thought

The key feature here is the *naturalistic fallacy*, described above in Chapter 3. If we can never argue from an 'is' to an 'ought', then any approach to language which tries to base meaning on evidence must automatically rule out the possibility of meaningful ethics.

It will now be clear why the logical positivist position was so threatening to ethics. If meaning is only given with respect to the evidence provided by the senses, then metaphysical ethics is meaningless, since it is based on abstract concepts that do not have a 'cash value' in terms of experience. But the attempt to escape from that charge and claim that morality is known through intuition is equally threatened. For if goodness and obligation cannot be 'reduced' to evidence of any sort, then – as far as the logical positivists were concerned – they too were meaningless. The positivists hoped to put language and meaning on the same sure basis as the physical sciences. Everything had to be tested out in terms of evidence: no evidence, no meaning.

But the positivist claim went further. Wittgenstein (and others) argued that *we can have no knowledge of private mental states*. They argued that to describe someone as angry, for example, did not imply that one had special access to a mental state. Rather, the word 'angry' describes someone who is red in the face, shouting, waving a fist in the air, and so on. Anger 'means' all that, because that is the only way in which I can specify why I used that word to describe that person. To take another example: an itch, on this theory, is merely a disposition to scratch. Wanting to scratch is what we call 'having an itch'.

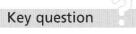**Key question**

Is it possible to have something called an 'itch', and yet not want to scratch it?

Faced with such criticism, attempts were made to find a meaning for religious language that would satisfy the criteria for meaningfulness set by logical positivism.

e) Emotivism

Key word

Emotivism: the view that ethical statements are merely expressions of approval or disapproval.

The criticism of moral statements by the logical positivists was based on the assumption that such statements were making factual claims. A. J. Ayer argued for a theory about the nature of ethical statements that became known as **emotivism**. An emotivist view gets round the logical positivist rules about what is meaningful by claiming that moral statements are not factual, but express the feelings of the person who makes them. If you like something then you call it 'good', if you dislike it, 'bad'. Thus two people can consider exactly the same facts and come to quite different moral conclusions. One cannot say that one is right or the other is wrong, because there are no facts that separate them, one can only accept that each is using moral judgements to express his or her emotional response to that set of facts.

Key question

How do emotions expressed in 'moral' statements differ (if at all) from other emotions?

This approach was taken by C. L. Stevenson in his *Ethics and Language* (1944). He was particularly concerned about how moral statements are used, and what results they are intended to produce. He claimed that the word 'good' was a *persuasive definition*: it was there to express your emotions. On the other hand, if you tried to go on from there to give some reason why you felt that way, that is more than emotivism will allow.

If moral statements are simply a listing of how we feel, that does not seem to do justice to the way in which moral statements are actually used. I may sense that, when I say of something that it is right or good, I am doing more than simply describing my emotions at the time. But what is that 'more'? To explore this, let us move to consider a second theory.

Key quote

'... in saying that a certain type of action is right or wrong, I am not making any factual statement, not even a statement about my own state of mind. I am merely expressing certain moral sentiments. And the man who is ostensibly contradicting me is merely expressing his moral sentiments. So there is plainly no sense in asking which of us is in the right. For neither of us is asserting a genuine proposition.'

A. J. AYER, *LANGUAGE, TRUTH AND LOGIC*, P.110F

f) Prescriptivism

Another approach to the same problem is to say that to make a moral statement is to prescribe a particular course of action. This approach was taken by R. M. Hare (*The Language of Morals* [1952] and *Freedom and Reason* [1963]). He argued that a moral statement is 'prescribing' a course of action, recommending that something should be done, not just expressing a feeling. On the other hand, moral statements are rather more than commands. A command is simply a request to do a particular thing at a particular moment, whereas a moral statement is making a more general suggestion about what action should be taken. In other words, a moral statement is both *prescriptive* and also *universalisable*: suggesting what everyone should do in the circumstances. Hare believed that, in this way, it was possible to apply reason and logic to matters of value.

Key quote

'If I ought to do this, then somebody else ought to do it to me in precisely similar circumstances.' So I have to ask myself: 'Am I prepared to prescribe that somebody else should do it to me in like circumstances?'

R. M. HARE (INTERVIEWED BY BRYAN MAGEE, *MEN OF IDEAS*, 1978)

Key word

Prescriptivism: the view that ethical statements prescribe a course of action.

Prescriptivism suggests that in responding to moral statements, we do not acknowledge that they are either true or false, but simply accept or reject the actions they are prescribing. Thus you may say to me 'It is right to feed those who are starving.' If I agree with that statement, what I am actually saying is 'Yes, that is a good policy; that is what I intend to do.'

All of this debate has come, of course, from the basic argument that you cannot derive an 'ought' from an 'is'. If (like the logical positivists) you believe that a statement only means something if you can point to evidence for it, where do you find your evidence for moral statements? Either in the area of human emotions expressed through them, or in the courses of action that such statements might prescribe – the first leads to emotivism and the second to prescriptivism.

Both theories avoid the claim that moral statements are meaningless, by pointing to the evidence of what actually happens when moral statements are made – for, whether or not they are meaningless in themselves, it is clear that moral statements do actually express emotions and recommend courses of action.

It is possible to argue that moral statements are means by which we overcome selfish perspectives. John Mackie (1917–1981), in *Ethics: Inventing Right and Wrong* (1977), argued that:

Key thought

Prescriptivist ethics follows a trend in linguistic philosophy in the first half of the twentieth century – away from a narrow, evidence-based sense of meaning towards an appreciation that the meaning of language is given by the way it is used.

- there are no objective moral values
- therefore all moral claims are objectively 'false'
- but we can continue to use moral language if it helps us to overcome narrow views and sympathies.

In other words, Mackie was building on the work of emotivism and prescriptivism by saying that morality has a function but not an objective basis.

On the other hand, there is a fundamental question to ask of this approach: Why not enjoy having limited sympathies? Why bother with moral codes at all? Why should it make any difference if our views are completely selfish or universally benevolent? *If we are 'inventing' right and wrong, why are we doing it? What does humankind have to gain from having developed a sense of conscience?* It would seem that at some point ethics needs to be based on something other than itself. Morality remains a phenomenon which needs some explanation.

Two issues relate to this, but are beyond the scope of this present book. The first is 'nihilism'. If there is no objective basis for ethical statements, and if they do no more than express our own preferences, then it is possible to argue that nothing whatever has inherent value. The second is that, if moral language simply refers to our present emotions or prescriptions, it is difficult to see how moral progress could be possible.

Key question

If morality is just expressing my preferences, what would it mean to say that I wanted to become a better person?

As was mentioned above (see page 38), much discussion of ethics from the turn of the century to the 1960s was concerned with the attempt to find some meaning for ethical language. We need to keep such discussion in mind as we move now to consider some traditional ethical theories. Traditional theories are more concerned with finding a basis for morality in experience, in emotions or in the way in which our minds work, than with the meaning of ethical language. In other words, they are concerned with the questions about 'What should I do?' and 'What is good?' rather than the secondary (meta-ethical) question 'What do I mean when I say that something is good?'

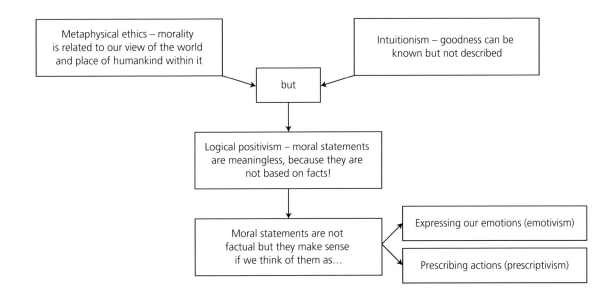

Study guide

By the end of this chapter you should have thought about the basic terms used in ethics, the impact of the logical positivist challenge to the meaningfulness of moral claims, and the responses to that challenge offered by emotivism and prescriptivism.

Revision checklist

Can you explain…?

- The difference between describing an action as moral, immoral or amoral.
- The difference between a deontological and the teleological approach to ethics.
- The distinctive feature of metaphysical ethics.

Do you know…?

- Why logical positivism challenged the meaningfulness of ethical language.
- Why emotivism and prescriptivism give meaning to ethical language while accepting the validity of the logical positivist challenge.

Give arguments for and against…

- The view that 'good' can be known but not defined.
- The logical positivist's view that moral statements are meaningless.

Revision activity

Most ethical questions are about specific moral issues and choices, but it is important, in responding to them, to be aware of the different theories of ethical language that may be used. Consider the following statements:

1 It is always wrong to kill another human being.

2 Do whatever you feel will help you to develop as an individual; don't simply be guided by what other people think of you.

3 You should always consider other people's feelings, rather than your own.

4 It is right to steal food, if that is the only way to stay alive.

For each of these, say how you would interpret and respond to the statement from the standpoint of the theories of moral language set out in this chapter. In each case, you should say also how you would decide whether or not to agree with it. In other words, take each of them and ask yourself 'How would an emotivist understand this, and how would he or she decide whether to agree with it or not?', then do the same for a prescriptivist. You should also think about whether the statements could be justified from the perspective of intuitionism or metaphysical ethics. A logical positivist would say that it is meaningless; would you agree?

Examples of essay questions

1. Moral statements are simply covert descriptions of emotions or recommendations for action. Discuss.

AO1 would require knowledge of the emotivist and prescriptivist approaches to ethical language. Higher level could include an acknowledgement of why these two approaches developed – that is in response to the accusation of meaninglessness from logical positivism.

For AO2, a good response might focus on the word 'simply', and consider whether there are elements in moral statements that cannot be covered by the two approaches that are outlined.

A more general question:

2. Does the emotive theory degrade ethical discussion?

Here, the AO1 element would simply require knowledge of the emotivist theory of moral claims, set against its background.

AO2 would be more difficult at this stage, but easier after covering later chapters in this book. Namely, it requires an assessment of the scope of what is achieved by ethical discussion, and whether that can be adequately appreciated by identifying it simply with the expression of emotions of approval or otherwise. Is such expression a 'degrading' of a full ethical argument, and – if so – what should also be involved in such an argument?

Further question

1 'Euthanasia is wrong.'
   Why might a logical positivist claim that it is a meaningless statement? Do you agree?

Chapter checklist

In this chapter we shall be concerned with the idea justice as it is explored within the *Republic,* and also with the idea of the 'Form of the Good', which underlies the whole of Plato's philosophy.

1 Introduction

Key people

Plato (c428–347BCE)
was born into a noble family in Athens, and much of his work shows an awareness of his political and social responsibilities, set against the background of the Greek city state (or *polis*). He was profoundly influenced by the philosopher Socrates, but when Socrates was condemned to death in 399BCE, Plato left Athens. He returned in 387BCE and founded the Academy, which may be considered the first university, by receiving students at his home.

Plato's writings generally take the form of dialogues (in which Socrates frequently appears as the principal character). They generally start with someone's claim to knowledge and the proposal of a definition of a key term. This is then scrutinised and tested by producing practical examples of its application, leading to the conclusion that the original definition was inadequate.

But when Plato discusses the meaning of justice, it is not merely the word 'justice' that is being considered, but the political reality that may be understood by that concept. Plato's early dialogues probably reflect the teachings of Socrates himself and generally follow the 'Socratic method' without appearing to present authoritative conclusions. Socrates made some fundamental points about virtue or morality, on which Plato was to build. They were:

- That virtue is knowledge: to know what is right is to do what is right.
- That all wrong-doing is the result of ignorance: nobody deliberately chooses to do what he or she knows to be wrong.
- That all virtues are fundamentally the same: you can't have one virtue but lack another.

In an early dialogue (*Gorgias*) Plato enquires about what constitutes a person's supreme good. He examines the claims that it is the ability to persuade people so that one could get exactly what one wanted, that it is the power of getting one's own way, and that it is the ability to satisfy all one's desires. None of these proves adequate.

Socrates argues that a person's desires are endless, and therefore that one can never achieve complete satisfaction simply by being given what one desires.

The dialogues of the middle period (including the *Republic*) still have Socrates as the principal character, but increasingly Plato moves beyond the traditional 'Socratic' form, and starts to expound his own ideas. There is also a change of emphasis, moving beyond ethical issues to examine the nature of reality itself. We have the development of his theory of 'Forms', in which Plato was to make a distinction between the appearance of things that are known to us through the senses, and underlying reality that makes them what they are, and which is known only through reason.

The problem with this (as pointed out by Alasdair MacIntyre in *A Short History of Ethics*, 1966) is that, on Plato's account, goodness and beauty are only known to a few educated individuals (those capable of understanding the underlying reality) whereas, in fact, everyone has *some* sense of what is good, for without it they would have nothing to desire or aspire to.

Key thought

Socrates argues that satisfaction can only be achieved if reason (rather than the appetites) decides what is to be desired.

2 Justice?

The *Republic* is concerned with what is meant by justice. It takes the form of a dialogue in which various definitions are proposed and examined, but then moves on to a more systematic exposition of Plato's views of the ideal state, the place of philosopher-rulers within it, the ethical principles needed to establish it, and the fundamental nature of reality which its rulers would need to understand in order to establish justice.

The proposal is presented by Thrasymachus, and then taken up by Glaucon and Adeimantus, that justice is what is in the interests of the stronger. Those who rule, in other words, determine what shall be considered just. There are differences between the proponents, in that Thrasymachus is crude in seeking to achieve his own ends in an obviously selfish way, whereas Glaucon and Adeimantus are prepared to be craftier and to accept moral principles and laws in order to achieve what they want in the long run.

They argue that, in a natural state, everyone is concerned for his or her own self-interest, but that society has to create a sense of order and justice in order to curb such self-interest for the benefit of others and to prevent total anarchy. People then obey the laws, since they fear the consequences of not doing so.

Key thought

If everyone seeks only their own self-interest, society breaks down. How then can you create a society in such a way that everyone achieves appropriate satisfaction? This is Plato's quest.

a) The ring of Gyges

But what if you could set aside all laws and act according to your own wishes and self-interest with guaranteed impunity? The story is told of the ring of Gyges, which had the power to make its wearer invisible. Given the opportunities afforded by such a ring, Gyges uses its power to achieve his own ends – in this case by seducing his queen and killing his king. The implication of the story is that, when all restraints and threats are removed, people will act in line with what they perceive to be their own self-interest.

3 Reason rules

Key thought

Plato argues that both the state and the individual should be ruled by reason.

Key words

Episteme: Greek term for knowledge.

Doxa: Greek term for opinion.

Key thought

There is a fundamental division in Plato's philosophy between eternal realities, which are known through reason, and the everyday world of particulars, which is known through sense experience. This influences both his *metaphysics* (i.e. his theory about what exists) and his *epistemology* (i.e. his theory about how we can know what exists). It is also key to understanding his approach to ethics; once he has established the importance of the eternal Forms, he moves on to the central idea for his ethics – the 'Form of the Good'.

Key word

Form: a universal reality, in which individual things share.

Key thought

If goodness and justice require reason, then philosophers alone are qualified to rule.

Plato considers a society in which everyone's needs are to be met. He suggests that it will involve three different classes of people: workers, to produce the goods needed for society; the military in order to defend the state; and rulers. Plato is convinced that people naturally fall into one or other of these three categories, and that it is best to divide the three functions between them, each taking what is most appropriate and sticking to that function alone.

So what makes a person a philosopher-king, capable of ruling the just state? Plato's answer is that the philosopher is able to have knowledge (*episteme*) as opposed to opinion (*doxa*). If, for example, you are aware that a particular thing is beautiful, that is merely opinion, and you may well not be able to say why it is beautiful. On the other hand, if you are aware of the nature of beauty itself, the very essence of beauty (the 'Form of the Beautiful') can become the object of knowledge, without depending upon particular examples.

a) Implications of this metaphysics

Plato's idea of goodness is transcendent – above and beyond any particular social conventions which concern people in their ordinary life. 'The Form of the Good' may be the source and inspiration for all other values, but it is a source that generally remains hidden.

This is relevant to Plato's ethics. Knowledge of the **Forms**, and particularly the Form of the Good is, for Plato, an end in itself. It gives meaning and purpose to life. And without some overall sense of meaning, moral considerations such as justice become meaningless. Just as Socrates had said that virtue is knowledge, so Plato argues here that to do what is right, and to order society justly, required knowledge of the 'Form of the Good', which is known through reason rather than experience.

Reference
Plato's account of 'The Cave' and further information about his metaphysics may be found in *Philosophy and Ethics* in this series.

4 The ideal state?

For Plato, there are three classes of people:

- the rulers (or guardians)
- the auxiliaries (or military)
- the workers.

In order to have a state where the rulers, the auxiliaries and the workers each perform their own functions, Plato recognises that there must be propaganda to the effect that those who are to be workers are born as such and must accept their lot. Equally he is concerned that there should be careful selection and education in order to provide the guardians needed to rule the state.

It is essential that there be inequality of opportunity and education for Plato's state to work. He takes fairly drastic action in order to implement it. There is to be selective breeding, so that the healthiest and most intellectually gifted are able to produce more children. Marriages are sanctioned by the state, for the purpose of creating gifted rulers. The ages for childbearing are set down, and although sex is freely permitted outside that age range, any children of such unions must be eliminated either by abortion or infanticide. Similarly, all deformed children must be removed from society.

Children are to be taken from their parents and brought up and educated together, so that they do not know who their parents are – and will therefore treat all adults with equal respect. Since children are not allowed to marry their own parents, all those whose age means that they could possibly be one's mother or father must be treated as such. In other words, in order to achieve the development of a ruling elite, Plato is prepared to sacrifice what others might see as fundamental individual rights and the natural family unit.

Once he establishes the means of training the guardians of his state, he has a system within which all three classes – guardians, auxiliaries and workers – know their place and work together in harmony.

a) The nature of the self in this scheme

Plato sees the three types of citizen in his state as corresponding to three aspects of the self – reason, will and appetite.

The base elements in the human self are the appetites, corresponding to the workers. Plato clearly wanted to make sure that they were controlled. The human 'will', or spirited nature, exhibits emotions and takes action, corresponding to the auxiliaries in the state. Then finally there is rational self, which sees the balance that is needed – the function of the rulers in a state.

Justice is achieved within the state when each class of people are able to perform their own function in harmony with the others. So

> **Key thought**
>
> Plato uses the analogy of the state to highlight three elements within the individual, with reason given the task of holding the appetites in check through the will.

> **Key thought**
>
> Plato outlines his ideal state, not because it is ever going to be possible to construct it, but simply in order to have a standard by which to judge actual states.

> **Key thought**
>
> For a balanced, moral life, the appetites should be controlled by reason, using the will to do so.

also in an individual, the rational part is there to control the appetites and also to guide the spirited or wilful part that expresses itself in bravery and action. All three are acknowledged, but they are set in a very definite hierarchy.

5 Why is it better to be just than unjust?

Plato offers three reasons for this:

Key question

Is it really better to be ruled by reason, rather than by your desires and your ability to pursue them (as Thrasymachus or Gyges)?

- A person who is unjust is ruled by his or her desires. But these are limitless and are therefore never to be satisfied – which results in frustration.
- If you know only your appetites, you are unable to judge between the benefits that reason can bring and those of the partial satisfaction of appetite. The philosopher, by contrast, knows both reason and appetite and is therefore in the best position to judge between them.
- Reason deals with the eternal truths and values, whereas satisfying the appetites is only a temporary way of staving off a sense of loss or dissatisfaction. Therefore the values of reason are always to be preferred.

Key questions

- Does the quest to satisfy the appetites inevitably lead to frustration?
- Is Plato right to have made this absolute distinction between reason and appetite? Do they actually work in opposition to one another as he suggests?

Key thought

Because, for Plato, justice depends on knowledge, there is the danger that it will be imposed by an intellectual elite upon a majority who are deemed to be incapable of understanding it.

What Plato is desperate to show is that a just man has greater satisfaction, no matter how much of a failure he might appear to be in worldly terms (remember Socrates!), but that the person who is driven to worldly success will always remain unfulfilled.

Towards the end of the *Republic*, Plato uses another myth, in which, after death, the just are rewarded and the unjust punished. Now this simply reflects his valuation of the two states, for it implies that the just deserve to be rewarded after death, rather than having justice as its own reward during this life. In a sense, therefore, the final myth does not actually contribute anything to Plato's argument for the inherent superiority of justice over injustice.

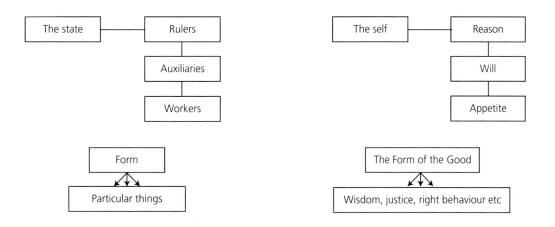

Study guide

By the end of this chapter you should understand Plato's vision of a world where the absolute reality is known only through reason, whereas particular things are known through experience, and in which – for that reason – it makes sense for philosophers to rule and establish justice, since they are deemed to have established within themselves the right balance between reason, will and appetite.

Revision checklist

Can you explain...?

- What Plato meant by a Form.
- Why the Forms are known only through reason, not experience.
- Why he believed only philosophers were able to establish justice.

Do you know...?

- The difference between *doxa* and *episteme*.
- The three divisions within the state and within the human self, and the parallels between them.

Give arguments for and against...

- Plato's claim that it is always better to be just (having one's life ordered by reason) than unjust.
- Plato's idea that society is best ruled by a small elite of intellectuals.

Example of essay questions

1. 'Knowledge automatically leads to virtue, and wrongdoing is the result of ignorance.' Discuss these ideas, which Plato ascribes to Socrates, saying whether or not you agree with Socrates, and illustrating your discussion with examples from one or more present-day situations.

AO1 would include an awareness of Plato's theory of the Forms, and the fact that – unlike experienced reality – they can be known only through reason. Higher level might also include knowledge that, for Plato, ignorance is displayed in not realising that the quest for satisfaction of appetites (which lies behind much wrongdoing) leads to frustration.

AO2 requires some sensitive assessment of the degree to which our behaviour is determined by reason rather than by our natural appetites and will. If it is argued that reason dominates, then it is reasonable to support Plato's case. If, on the other hand, it is argued that we are basically creatures of appetite and will, then it is more difficult to sustain the claim that wrongdoing is the result of ignorance. For higher level, examples will be given to illustrate and support the particular line of argument.

Further questions

1 It is better to be just than unjust. Discuss.

2 Given the chance, people will always act in their own self-interest. Do you agree?

6 ARISTOTLE AND HAPPINESS

Chapter checklist ✓

In this chapter we shall explore Aristotle's idea of 'happiness' as the good to which all life aspires, looking also at the Epicurean and Stoic responses to his thought.

1 The quest for *eudaimonia*

In the opening of his *Nicomachean Ethics*, Aristotle (384–322BCE) makes a basic statement upon which his ethics is to depend:

> *Every craft and every investigation, and likewise every action and decision, seems to aim at some good; hence the good has been well described as that at which everything aims.*

What is meant by 'good' here is a goal or purpose, something that is wanted for its own sake and not for the sake of something else. Aristotle seeks 'the good', the best of goods, and he finds it in the idea of *eudaimonia*, which is generally translated as 'happiness'. He sees happiness as the fundamental goal of life because of the way in which it relates to other goals. For whereas he sees honour, pleasure and understanding as valid goals in themselves, he thinks that people also pursue them because they believe that they will find happiness in doing so. By contrast, he argues that nobody pursues happiness for the sake of something else. Thus happiness is a goal that lies beneath and holds together the other valid goals that a person may choose. In itself it makes life worthwhile.

The English word 'happiness' does not really convey what Aristotle meant by *eudaimonia*. Aristotle used it to describe a situation in which a person both experienced life as going well (our usual meaning of happiness) and also behaved well. In other words, *eudaimonia* included the idea of virtue. Now virtue is not simply a state in which one finds oneself, rather it is a disposition to act in a certain way. A person is called virtuous if, given certain

Key word

Eudaimonia: Greek term for 'happiness'.

Key thought

It makes sense to say 'I want to be X in order to be happy' but nobody is going to say 'I want to be happy in order to be X.'

Key quote

'... we regard something as self-sufficient when all by itself it makes a life choiceworthy and lacking nothing; and that is what we think happiness does.'

NICOMACHEAN ETHICS, BOOK 1

Key question

Should you strive for virtue, and believe that happiness will follow? Why should we assume that they go together? What of the person who is virtuous but miserable?

Key quote

'Good itself will be no more of a good by being eternal; for a white thing is no whiter if it lasts a long time than if it lasts a day.'

NICOMACHEAN ETHICS

circumstances, he or she can be expected to act in a way that is kindly, generous, moral etc. One of the problems for ethics is how virtue is related to happiness. And if they do not inevitably go together, which should you aim for, virtue or happiness? We shall look at these issues a little later. For now, we need to note that Aristotle included both in his concept of *eudaimonia*.

What should be absolutely clear, however, is that when Aristotle makes 'happiness' the goal of life, he is *not* equating it with pleasure. In section 5 of Book 1 of the *Nicomachean Ethics* he claims that there are three types of life: of gratification, of political activity and of study. Of the first, his contempt is clear:

> *The many, the most vulgar, seemingly conceive the good and happiness as pleasure, and hence they also like the life of gratification. Here they appear completely slavish, since the life they decide on is a life for grazing animals.*

The second is important, for he sees ethics in the context of the involvement in the life of the *polis* (the city state), but the last – the life of study – he regards most highly.

Notice that, when a person seeks happiness, it is something that (potentially at least) belongs to this world; it is a state that is imaginable, not some impossible ideal. Aristotle disagrees with Plato's view that the Form of the Good is something eternal, of which individual good things here are mere copies. Goodness is goodness – what we see here is the real thing, not some pale reflection. What is more, our concerns are with particular things we experience, not with abstract entities. To use Aristotle's own example, a doctor needs to understand the health of his patient, not some abstract idea of 'health'.

What is your idea of 'the good life'? A holiday apartment by a pool? Leisure? Is that sufficient to make life worthwhile? *Eudaimonia* is not just another term for pleasure, but emphasises both 'living well' and 'doing well'.

Reason

Aristotle made the crucial distinction between material substance and form. What makes you a human being is not the individual bits of flesh and bone of which you are comprised (material substance), but the overall way in which all such material is organised to make you a living person (form). Aristotle said that the soul was the 'form' of the body – in other words, one's soul was the shape and meaning and purposeful direction of one's life. He then argued that the distinctive human quality was reason. It is the ability to think that sets humankind apart from all other things, and therefore reason becomes the supreme human virtue.

So reason is needed in order to be fully human. But, for Aristotle, reason was not just the faculty of thinking, which could be developed simply by being instructed in logic, but included a moral sense. In other words, human reason included the idea of obeying the precepts of reason, putting into practice what one intellectually judged to be good.

Reason, therefore, involves understanding, responding and choosing. And that is why reason is related closely to *eudaimonia*. Human excellence consists in making choices, based on practical reason, which will lead to the overall goal of humankind, which is *eudaimonia* – happiness.

For Aristotle, the unique feature of human life is reason, and therefore actions are to be judged in the light of reason. It is reason that leads people to seek their chosen end (their **telos**) and the ability to think about actions and match them up with a chosen telos is *phronesis* (prudence).

The ideal human *telos*, therefore, would seem to be to live the life of a Greek gentleman philosopher – Aristotle's 'great-souled man'. He is:

- rational
- balanced
- good company among his equals
- independent.

His chosen end is *eudaimonia* – to live well and to fulfil himself by behaving in a way that demonstrates the highest human quality, rationality. If he develops a friendship with someone it is for a purpose – because it is useful or pleasant – rather than being friendship for its own sake. If Plato's 'Form of the Good' were considered a remote and other worldly goal, then Aristotle's 'great-souled man' is very much a worldly, self-satisfied and culturally conditioned alternative.

Key thought

Notice here an important thread that runs from Socrates, through Plato to Aristotle. The faculty of reason is not merely one of understanding, but also one of action: *ethics is reason put into practice*. It is very important to keep this in mind, since there are some approaches to ethics in which human reason alone is not a sufficient basis for morality.

Key word

Telos: Greek term for 'end' or 'purpose'.

Key thought

Of all the actions that are pleasant, Aristotle sees intellectual reasoning as the highest, for it contemplates truths that are timeless. A person who is engaged in such reasoning is superior to another who lives life dominated by emotion, or who behaves simply out of hope of reward or the avoidance of punishment.

2 The mean

Key word

The mean: Aristotle's idea that
doing right involves a balance
between extremes

Key quote

'For the man who flies from and
fears everything and does not
stand his ground against anything
becomes a coward, and the man
who fears nothing at all but goes
to meet every danger becomes
rash... [courage is]... destroyed by
excess and defect, and preserved
by the mean.'

NICOMACHEAN ETHICS, BOOK 2

Key quote

'But not every action nor every
passion admits of a mean; for
some have names that already
imply badness, e.g. spite,
shamelessness, envy, and in the
case of actions adultery, theft,
murder; for all of these and
suchlike things imply by their
names that they are themselves
bad and not the excesses or
deficiencies of them.'

NICOMACHEAN ETHICS, BOOK 6

The most problematic aspect of Aristotle's ethics is his idea of **the
mean.** He argued that – in the case of both emotions and actions –
the difference between virtue and vice was a matter of balance or
extremes. To take one of his examples, he says that jealousy is a vice
because one becomes upset by the good fortune of another person,
even if that good fortune is deserved. On the other hand, he
considers it quite reasonable to become indignant at the good
fortune of another person if that good fortune is undeserved. In
other words, to be righteously indignant is fine, as long as it is held
in balance. If it is taken to the extreme, it becomes jealousy and
therefore a vice.

A possible implication of this view is that emotions and actions
are morally neutral in themselves; it is only an extreme form of
them which counts as a vice. A criticism of Aristotle on this point
(for example, by Alasdair MacIntyre) is that there are some
emotions, such as malice, and some actions, such as theft or murder,
which are inherently evil. It is not quite that simple however, since
the term 'murder' indicates that the situation is extreme. To practise
capital punishment or killing people in war would then be
considered a balanced reason for carrying out the same act of taking
a life. But Aristotle already takes this into account, as the quote
opposite shows.

What Aristotle's theory does not appear to take into account,
however, are the circumstances in which an action is performed or
emotion experienced. But (to use our existing example) it is these,
rather than the act itself, that turn lawful killing into murder.
Aristotle, of course, saw reason as paramount. Perhaps it would
therefore be better to say that Aristotle's idea of the mean is that a
reasonable and appropriate action should be judged a virtue and an
extreme (and therefore unreasonable) one should be judged a vice.

a) Doing well and doing what is right

It is important to keep in mind the distinction, made by Alasdair
MacIntyre in his *Short History of Ethics*, between the Greek idea of
morality in terms of 'faring well' and the modern view of morality
as 'doing right'. Modern ethics seeks to know what is right or
wrong without linking those terms overtly to the quality of life that
they offer. That is not the case with Aristotle – his ethics are aimed
squarely at the good life, in which happiness and virtue, blending
into a range of virtues exemplified by the life of the philosopher, are
set up as the ultimate criterion by which to judge all human action.

But when it comes to discussions about how to achieve the good
life, Aristotle argued that people already have in their minds the
'end' to which they aim. The problems they face concern the best

Key thought

Some Protestant Christians take the view that human nature is 'fallen' and therefore that people's natural inclinations are bound to be wrong. Hence morality cannot be based on 'faring well'. This was particularly true of Kant (see Chapter 10), who has been so influential in ethics. He saw morality as being a matter for pure practical reason, independent of one's experience or the expected results of an action. Not so for the Greeks. Their concern with ethics was to see how people could live well.

Key quote

'We deliberate not about ends but about means. For a doctor does not deliberate whether he shall heal, nor an orator whether he shall persuade, nor a statesman whether he shall produce law and order, nor does any one else deliberate about his end. They assume the end and consider how and by what means it is to be attained; and if it seems to be produced by several means they consider by which it is most easily and best produced, while if it is achieved by one only they consider how it will be achieved…'

NICOMACHEAN ETHICS,
BOOK 3, SECTION 3

means of achieving that end. In other words, people need to discuss those things that are within their power to change, but all such discussions imply an 'end' that the person has in mind. Now, this raises the same issue as intuitionism (see above page 39), which claims fundamental concepts such as goodness and beauty are beyond rational debate. Aristotle seems to imply that our chosen 'end' is something that we just have in the back of our minds, informing (but not part of) the practical choices we make. This may lead us to ask: Is ethics about the goals people have, or the means they employ to achieve them?

b) The context

The qualities that Aristotle judges to be virtues – courage, temperance, gentleness, liberality, wittiness, magnificence, being agreeable in company – show that the norm of behaviour that he considers is that of the freeman within the upper classes of Greek society. In the end, although he does not state it in quite these blunt terms, Aristotle's ethics comes to the view that the highest good to which one can aspire is to be like… Aristotle!

In summing up the Greek contribution to ethics, Alasdair MacIntyre (in his *Short History of Ethics*) makes the important point that the work of Plato and Aristotle needs to be seen against the background of the decline of the *polis*. Whereas Plato thought that philosophers would make ideal rulers, Aristotle sees their prime function as thinking and contemplating, rather than getting directly involved in political life, thus disengaging ethics from its political matrix. His was a time (particularly under his pupil, Alexander the Great) when the smaller city states were to give way to larger political monarchies and empires. In such a situation, power and decision-making are focused in the individual monarch, and other people become citizens of the state. Thus as we move on from the time of Plato and Aristotle, we find that morality is far more concerned with the individual, and the political aspects of ethics mainly concern the relationship between the individual and the state.

3 The Epicureans

Key thought

With the Epicureans, ethics starts to be concerned with the individual and his or her place in the universe. How that relates to the relative place of people within society becomes a secondary matter – politics, sociology and ethics have separated themselves out.

Named after Epicurus, Epicurean philosophy took as its starting point the idea that the whole world was composed of impersonal atoms, controlled by physical laws. They did not see the universe as a moral place, but as entirely neutral. If people choose to behave morally, that fact does not reflect any universal structure, but is simply a choice made by humans for their own particular ends.

Like Aristotle, they saw that morality involved making choices in order to achieve a chosen end. They saw that end as human

Key people

Epicurus (341–270BCE)
was a materialist, believing that the universe comprised atoms in space. In an unpredictable world, he sought to free people from the fear of death (death is nothing, since we are not there to experience it), and encouraged them to live with modest enjoyment. He set up communities (open to all, even slaves and women – radical in his day) in which people could live out his philosophy.

Key thought

In small quantities, alcohol appears to offer pleasure, but as intake increases it leads to sickness and ultimately death. Prudently restricting the appetite for more and more alcohol offers longer-term benefits.

pleasure, although they regarded the virtues as the art of achieving it. In other words, you might well restrain your inclinations, but that was only because unrestrained inclinations can lead eventually to more pain than pleasure. Restraint is applied in order to achieve longer-term happiness.

Notice however that the basis of ethics has changed. For Plato, ethics was based very much on a person's place within the social and political life of the Greek city state. For Aristotle, the criteria became more general but also more individualistic. Qualities that make for social harmony were regarded as virtues not because they made for social harmony, but because they ultimately benefited the individual. The great-souled man is independent – or rather, if he does depend on the help of slaves to maintain his lifestyle, he does not take that into account in his moral thinking! By contrast, with the Epicureans, we find a moral theory that is related to an individual's chosen end, within an impersonal and morally neutral universe.

All the conventional virtues are still accepted, but they are now a means to an end – human happiness – rather than an end in themselves or for reasons of society.

Key features for an Epicurean approach:

- the physical world is impersonal
- seek your own happiness by living modestly.

4 The Stoics

Key word

Stoics: members of a philosophical movement, named after the Stoa Poikile (painted colonnade) in Athens, where Zeno gave his lectures.

Key people

Zeno (c.334–262BCE)
Founder of the Stoic school of philosophy, Zeno moved from his native Cyprus to Athens to study and stayed on there to lecture. He considered that the best way of life was one lived in harmony with the rational ordering of the universe. Accepting what cannot be changed, calming the emotions and living a simple life, he sought a life based on reason.

The **Stoic** school of philosophy, founded by Zeno, took a view of the universe and of ethics that was quite different from that of the Epicureans. As a philosophy, it was influential in later Roman thought, where its exponents included Seneca (1–65CE), Epictetus (50–130CE) and the Emperor Marcus Aurelius, whose *Meditations* are a good source of information about Stoic views.

The Stoics believed that the universe was ordered by divine providence, that there was a fundamental principle (the *logos*) which determined everything that happened, and that – by definition – the *logos* was good. Since everything, including one's own future welfare, was determined by a morally good agent, it made no sense to seek happiness as the goal of life. Rather, they sought to live in a way that fitted in with the overall, rational plan of the universe, and hoped that happiness might follow.

In this sense, the Stoics came closer to modern views of morality than either the Epicureans or Aristotle. They held that what counted was to make an effort to act morally, irrespective of the consequences, and to act through reason rather than through

Key word

Logos: Greek for 'word', the universal rational principle in Stoic thought.

Key people

Marcus Aurelius (121–180CE)
Demonstrating that a Roman Emperor can also be a philosopher, he was the last great writer of the Stoic school. His *Meditations* are personal reflections on life, but also serve as a wonderful introduction to Stoic thought and practice.

Key quotes

'Do not seek to have events happen as you want them to, but instead want them to happen as they do happen, and your life will go well.'

EPICTETUS *ENCHIRIDION* NOTE 8

That sounds a rather negative view (hope for nothing and you will not be disappointed), but in fact, there is a good reason Epictetus takes this line:

'You are foolish if you want your children and your wife and your friends to live for ever, since you are wanting things to be up to you that are not up to you, and things to be yours that are not yours. You are stupid in the same way if you want your slave boy to be faultless, since you are wanting badness not to be badness but something else... Whoever want to be free, therefore, let him not want or avoid anything that is up to others. Otherwise he will necessarily be a slave.'

NOTE 14 (BOTH QUOTES FROM CAHN [ED.] *CLASSICS OF WESTERN PHILOSOPHY*)

emotion. Such morality they considered to be the only 'good' and immorality the only 'evil'.

The natural ethical response to the Stoic's sense of universal order, was to act with integrity, since the human soul was thought to be part of a wider world soul. Every human action is controlled by universal laws, but where we are free to make a choice we should be aware of the part we are called to play within the overall scheme of things. If you do what is right, you are at one with the basic reason that guides the whole universe. That, and that alone, is the basis of morality. Exclude any thoughts of personal gain, or the promptings of the emotions, act in tune with the universe and do what is right, leaving the final outcome to God.

Key features for a Stoic approach:

- Recognise reality for what it is, and do not pretend it is different.
- Take responsibility for what is up to you, not for what is not up to you.
- There is a universal order determining events.
- What matters is not the result of action (that is not up to you) but the act of will to do what is right.

Notice the important shift that has taken place. Aristotle spoke of the purpose or end (*telos*) to which every act tends. He saw happiness (*eudaimonia*) as that end for humankind. In the end a person sought what was in his or her own best interest, allowing for the fact that virtue would contribute to that 'happiness'. The Stoics went on to give a universal structure that would give virtue a value quite apart from any individual happiness that might arise because of it. For the Stoics, it was useless to build morality on possible results, because they would always be uncertain. Morality therefore had to stand on its own feet, as an end in itself, and as an expression in the individual will of the universal rational principle that orders everything.

Such Stoic attitudes, blended with the newly growing Christian religion, suggested a place for morality within the divine scheme for the universe – something we find particularly in the work of the medieval philosopher and theologian Aquinas. This approach can be termed 'natural law'; in other words, everything has an overall rational purpose within the universe, and that recognition of that purpose is a basis for moral action.

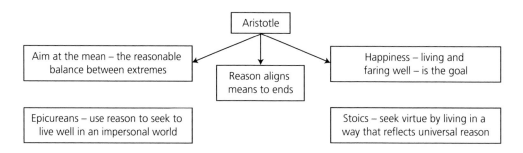

Study guide

By the end of this chapter you should have an understanding of what Aristotle meant by *eudaimonia* and the mean. You should also have thought about the way that the Epicureans and Stoics made important shifts from Aristotle's ethical theory.

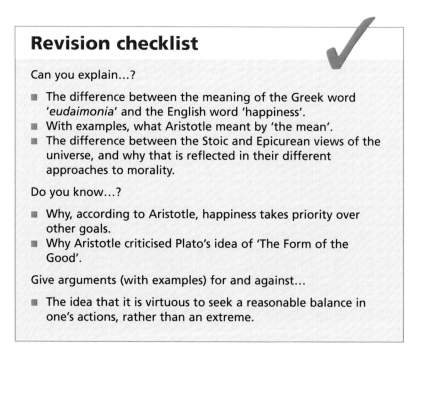

Revision checklist

Can you explain...?

- The difference between the meaning of the Greek word '*eudaimonia*' and the English word 'happiness'.
- With examples, what Aristotle meant by 'the mean'.
- The difference between the Stoic and Epicurean views of the universe, and why that is reflected in their different approaches to morality.

Do you know...?

- Why, according to Aristotle, happiness takes priority over other goals.
- Why Aristotle criticised Plato's idea of 'The Form of the Good'.

Give arguments (with examples) for and against...

- The idea that it is virtuous to seek a reasonable balance in one's actions, rather than an extreme.

Examples of essay questions

1. Do you consider eudaimonia to be the good at which everyone aims? Give your reasons.

AO1 would require a knowledge of the scope of the term *eudaimonia*, and the higher level might explore the reason why Aristotle gives it priority.

AO2 would then tease out whether you consider 'living well' in that broad sense to be what morality is about, and whether it is realistic for everyone to aim at it.

2. Aristotle's ideal person would be smug. Discuss.

For AO1, this essay question gives an opportunity to look at the whole background to Aristotle, and to the ideal of being a well-rounded individual. It also gives scope to examine what modern people consider to be a moral life, and how it relates to the idea of living well.

For AO2, it might be questioned whether this is the sort of ethics that would make sense to a slave, for example. It could also involve discussing whether being justifiably self-satisfied is in itself a moral failing.

Further questions

1 a) Explain with examples Aristotle's concept of 'the mean'.
   b) Do you consider Aristotle's idea of 'the mean' to be an adequate way of evaluating right and wrong?
   c) When would it be right not to seek a 'mean'?

2 The moral philosophy of the Epicureans and Stoics added little, if anything, to that of Aristotle. Discuss.

Chapter checklist

In this chapter we will examine the natural law approach to ethics, as set out by Aquinas, with an assessment of its strengths and weaknesses, and some indication of how it is applied.

Aquinas wrote from within the Christian tradition, and sought to present a rational basis for Christian morality. In doing this, he was profoundly influenced by Aristotle, whose work was beginning to be examined and taught again in European universities in the thirteenth century. The result of this fusion of the secular philosophy of Aristotle and the religious tradition of the Catholic Church produced what is known as the natural law approach to ethics, a version of which had already been developed by the Stoics.

1 Two approaches to Christian morality

Key people

Thomas Aquinas (1225–74) was born in Roccasecca, Italy, and studied in the universities of Naples, Cologne and Paris. As a member of the Dominican order, his life was committed to study and preaching. Combining Aristotle's philosophy with Christian doctrine and morality, his approach to ethics has been hugely influential within the Catholic Church. Of his total output of about 8 million words, his major works include *Summa Theologiae* and *Summa contra Gentiles*.

There are two very different approaches to morality from the perspective of Christianity: the first is based on the authority of revelation and the other – which we examine in this chapter – on natural law.

a) The authority of revelation

It is possible to see Christian morality as based on revelation and therefore quite independent of any rational ethical theories. This view takes the scriptures (as interpreted by the Church), the authority of Church leaders and the inspiration of the Holy Spirit as sources of authority. By contrast, it may see any system of morality based on human reason as of very limited value. This stems from the theological conviction that, through the 'Fall' in the Garden of Eden, all natural human life, including human reason, is separated from God through sin, unable to know and respond to God's will.

This approach (which has developed in the main within the Protestant traditions) sees no point in trying to use human reason as the basis for ethics; rather, all Christian morality comes through the revelation of God himself. This approach was taken at the Reformation by Luther, and in the twentieth century it is found in Protestant writers such as Bonhoeffer (see his *Ethics*, 1949).

b) Natural law

The natural law approach, by contrast, takes as its starting point Aristotle's idea that everything has a purpose, revealed in its design (or natural 'form'), and that the fulfilment of that design is the supreme 'good' to be sought. This approach did not claim that Christian morality could be based on human reason alone, or could operate without any input from revelation. Rather, it argued that human reason (given by God) was a starting point for morality. Reason could offer a logical basis for those moral precepts that were also known through revelation, and which could be supplemented by the specific moral rules presented in the Scriptures.

This was seen as a particularly valuable approach where moral dilemmas occurred for which there was no biblical precedent, and for which there was therefore no obviously relevant principle given by revelation. The natural law approach dominates Catholic moral thinking.

2 Final causes

Key words

Efficient cause: the agent that brings something about.

Final cause: the final aim or purpose of something.

Aristotle makes an important distinction between an **efficient cause** and a **final cause**. An efficient cause is the agent of change which brings about its effect – in other words, it is what we would normally call a 'cause' and is what science is concerned with. If we ask 'Why did the car skid off the road?' we want to know about the road surface, the state of the car's tyres and so on. In other words, we are looking for those things in existence immediately prior to whatever we are examining, which contributed to it happening. That is a question of 'efficient causes'. On the other hand, if I ask 'Why is that abstract sculpture shaped that way?' I do not look for an answer in terms of the way the sculptor angled his chisel, or the specific order in which material was cut away from the original block. Rather, I am interested in the concept in the sculptor's mind – the purpose and aim that explains why the sculpture is as it is. That purpose is the 'final cause' of the sculpture.

Now we can examine the whole universe in terms of 'efficient causation'. We look for the sequence of events that brings about a particular result. But that leaves out of account any sense of overall design or purpose – any 'final cause'. The natural law argument

Key thought

Natural law is therefore based on a rational interpretation of purposiveness within the world, not simply on an objective account of what is in fact the case.

depends upon this distinction. It assumes that – by whatever means employed – the world is the creation of God, and that it should therefore reveal his purpose in creating it.

This is how Aquinas links the general Aristotelian idea of agents and end, with the Christian idea of God as creating a purpose for everything:

> *Now everything that is produced through the will of an agent is direct-ed to an end by that agent: because the good and the end are the proper object of the will, wherefore whatever precedes from a will must needs be directed to an end…*
>
> *Consequently God, who in Himself is perfect in every way, and by His power endows all things with being, must needs be the Ruler of all, Himself ruled by none…*
>
> *[For] some things are so produced by God that, being intelligent, they bear a resemblance to Him and reflect His image: wherefore not only are they directed, but they direct themselves to their appointed end by their own actions.*
>
> (*Summa Contra Gentiles* Book 3, section 1)

In other words, human beings, since they are intelligent, are able to direct themselves and therefore take responsibility for knowing and doing what God intends for them. Therefore, human reason is required to examine and follow the sense of purpose that, according to Aquinas, God gives the world by virtue of being its creator.

Key thought

THE 'LAW OF DOUBLE-EFFECT'

Directing yourself with a goal in mind can be problematic. Sometimes, doing something with the intention of bringing about a good effect may have secondary consequences that are bad. In such cases, the 'law of double-effect' says that you are justified by your intended good effect, even if there is also a bad secondary effect, but you would not be justified in doing something bad, for the sake of a beneficial secondary effect.

3 Features of 'natural law'

- Natural law can refer simply to the observed laws of nature. In this sense it is simply a matter of science, which was originally called 'natural philosophy'. This is *not* what the natural law argument is based on, since it is quite possible to look at the 'efficient' causes of things without seeing any sense of 'good' or purpose or design within them.

- As presented by Aquinas, the natural law approach is based on the religious conviction that God created the world, establishing within it a sense of order and purpose that reflects his will.
- If everything is created for a purpose, human reason, in examining that purpose, is able to judge how to act in order to conform to that purpose.
- In the natural law approach to ethics, an action is judged solely on whether it conforms to a rational interpretation of its purpose within nature. It does not depend for its moral justification upon any results. Thus an action can be deemed morally good in itself, even if it brings about suffering.
- Since natural law is based on reason rather than revelation, it is in principle discoverable by anyone, whether religious or not. For the same reason, it is universal, rather than limited to any one culture or religion.

Key thought

SELF-DEFENCE

It is natural for a creature to want to defend itself against any threat to its life. This is justified on a natural law approach, since one cannot fulfil one's 'final cause' without being able to live to do so. Natural law therefore accepts the right of self-defence and equally argues for the preservation of innocent human life.

Key question

IS IT RIGHT TO KILL AND EAT ANIMALS?

If their 'final cause' is to be food for humans, then it is right according to a natural law approach. If their final cause is to flourish as animals, it would seem that killing them off frustrated that purpose, and may therefore be considered wrong.

An obvious and widely discussed application of the natural law argument within the Catholic Church concerns the purpose of sex and the implications this has for contraception:

- Clearly, the 'final cause' of the sexual act is the procreation of children.

What is it for? What does it do? Actually, it helps you take the screw caps off jars. It is designed for that specific purpose, and would be hopeless if used as a toothpick or comb! According to natural law, everything has a natural purpose and it is judged 'good' by fulfilling it.

Key thought

If we interpret the world as a place where everything has a 'final cause' or purpose
Then we can decide what is right or wrong accordingly
But if there is no 'final cause', there is no means of judging any one thing to be more appropriate than another.

- The 'efficient cause' of the sexual act is the erotic attraction and stimulation that makes the act both desirable and possible.
- But that attraction and stimulation arises because of biological processes that have developed in order to encourage suitable breeding. The individual may not experience that sexual drive in terms of producing children, but that is its biological origin.
- Therefore, whatever the actual experience and intentions of those engaging in the act of intercourse, the 'final cause' is clearly related to the conceiving of children.
- The natural law approach therefore argues that any action taken to frustrate that natural end is morally wrong.
- This is not negated by the argument that within nature the vast majority of sperm never fertilise an egg, since each sperm is designed with the fertilising of an egg as its goal, even if it does not actually succeed in doing so.
- Hence the natural law argument would see contraception, homosexuality and masturbation as inherently wrong, since they cannot lead to the 'final end' of sexuality in conception.

The natural law approach to ethics can claim to have an advantage over one which is based on the expected results of an action, namely that results cannot always be predicted, and can never be fully assessed. By contrast, this theory declares an act to be right or wrong quite apart from its consequences. The act can therefore be assessed morally prior to acting, and (provided that the natural law argument has been correctly applied) it is difficult to see how that assessment can later be overturned. It may also claim the advantage of being rationally based, and therefore not dependent upon the feelings of the person concerned. Feelings can change, but the issue of right and wrong remains fixed.

On the other hand, like many arguments, the natural law argument is vulnerable in terms of its presuppositions. It takes as its starting point belief in the purposive nature of the natural world. In its earlier Stoic form, it saw reason (in the form of the *logos*) as an inherent feature of the universe; in its Christian form it saw the world as the product of a purposeful creator God. If, faced with the apparent meaninglessness of events on a cosmic scale, or the purposelessness of innocent suffering, one comes to the conclusion that the universe does not conform to the expectations of human reason, or that it is unlikely to be the product of an omnipotent or loving creator, then the natural law argument loses its foundation.

a) Casuistry

Casuistry is the term used for the process whereby the general principles of natural law are applied to specific cases, and it is used generally for any system that starts with fixed principles and then

Key words

Probabilism: applying moral principles to situations is not an exact science. Within the Catholic Church, probabilists hold that a sufficient body of authoritative opinion (e.g. five or six theologians) is required in order to establish the solid probability that a judgement is correct.

Equiprobabilism: if two different moral views are almost equally probable, the equiprobabilist argues that either can be followed with a good conscience.

Key thought

These cardinal virtues link natural law to virtue ethics (see Chapter 16). These two ethical theories are like two sides of a coin. To achieve one's 'final cause' may require virtues, which themselves produce human flourishing and make life worthwhile.

Key thought

As a theory, natural law depends on reason. It has become a basis for religious (particularly Catholic) morality through the belief that the world as been created by God and therefore reflects His will and purpose, discernable by reason.

applies them logically to individual situations. The word 'casuistry' tends to have a pejorative sense, in that a moral assessment based on it can depend upon the skill of the person who is arguing the case for or against. It can therefore be caricatured as insensitive and authoritarian, although in practice its authority is modified according to a principle known as **probabilism**. On the other hand, it should be recognised that any system of ethics that is going to make any claim to universal or absolute principles is going to involve some form of casuistry.

b) The cardinal virtues

In *Summa Theologica*, Aquinas sets out four human qualities which reflect the moral life: *prudence, justice, fortitude* and *temperance*. These are known as the four cardinal virtues (the word 'cardinal' comes from *cardo*, meaning a hinge), and they were taken by the Stoics as the basis of the moral life. They also feature in both Plato and Aristotle. They represent the human qualities that reason suggests are required in order to live a moral life and to achieve the 'final cause' that reason sees as the overall purpose in life. The opposite of these cardinal virtues are the seven capital vices: *pride, avarice, lust, envy, gluttony, anger and sloth* – often referred to as the 'seven deadly sins'.

Notice that these virtues and vices, as they appear in Aquinas, are based on reason and on the sense of purpose in life. They stand independent of any specifically Christian revelation. Thus, for example, the cardinal virtues might be contrasted with the theological virtues – faith, hope and love – which appear in the New Testament.

c) Theology and reason

Natural law arguments are generally associated with Christian moral thought, particularly within the Catholic tradition. They are connected with issues of authority and with Canon Law (see page 132). On the other hand, natural law is based on reason rather than authority and is a development of Greek, and particularly Stoic principles.

Notice that the Lutheran and other Protestant theological positions may argue against depending principally on the natural law approach to ethics, on the grounds that it gives to humankind a moral status independent of God's grace. They believe that any such status undermines the belief that salvation comes through God's grace, rather than by keeping moral rules. On the other hand, some might want to argue that the natural law approach is a first step – a level of morality that can be shared with those who are non-believers.

There is another important point to be recognised here. We saw earlier that it is very basic to ethics that an 'ought' cannot be derived from an 'is' (page 30). But clearly that is what the natural law argument is doing; it is setting up moral norms based on a perceived sense of purpose within the natural order. But there is one important factor to be taken into account, namely that in natural law the view of the universe as purposeful is not given in terms of sense experience, rather it is an *interpretation* of that experience. The fact that something has a 'final cause' or purpose is not given directly as part of the experience of that thing, rather it is the interpretation that the rational mind gives to its place in the whole scheme of things. Hence the perception of morality in natural law is simply the application to individual situations of that overall perception of a purposeful world.

d) Natural rights

If natural law is about the end of purpose of human life, we should expect that there are features of life that are essential, so that supporting them is a way to ensure human fulfilment. In *Natural Law and Natural Rights* (OUP, 1980), John Finnis argues that natural rights are all valuable in themselves, self-evident, and should not be traded off against one another. He then argues that one should act in ways that allow integral human fulfilment.

Finnis' natural rights:

- Life
- Knowledge
- Play
- Beauty
- Friendship
- Practical reasonableness
- Religion

This move towards specifying the human 'goods' is useful in that it gives a clearer picture of what human fulfilment – our 'final cause' – is about. It also brings natural law closer to the situation where there are legal and political choices to be made. So, in arguing that the principal responsibility of a ruler is to seek the common good, one gets a clearer idea of what people require for the good life, and therefore what needs to be done to bring it about.

Another advantage of this position is that it does not *require* belief in God for its validity. As with virtue ethics (see p.152), it is possible to base natural law on the concept of human fulfilment and flourishing.

e) The attempt to integrate perception, with its limitations

When we move on to consider other ethical theories, we shall see that some are based on expected results (utilitarianism), others on emotion (English moralism), and others on a radical separation of the human will or human development from any external facts about the universe (a line of argument that will take us from Kant, through Nietzsche to existentialism). In contrast to all of these,

Key people

John Finnis (b. 1940)
is Professor of Law at the University of Oxford. He is a major figure in promoting a modern form of the natural law approach to law and to ethics, and his work has provoked major discussion about the basis for law.

natural law is the attempt to use human reason to relate ethics to the general structure of the universe. Aquinas' *Summa Theologica* is a drawing together of metaphysics (the branch of philosophy that considers what is real), ethics and religion. It is a monumental attempt to find an overarching way of integrating one's whole perception of reality, humankind's place within it, and the moral implications of that place.

There are however some fundamental problems with any natural law approach:

Key question

Death may be the natural result of illness. So, if morality is based on a rational interpretation of nature, should we ever try to prolong the life of someone who is seriously ill?

- How do we know what is natural? Should we judge it according to the natural outworking of physical laws?
- What happens when specific religious moral injunctions conflict with the more general principles that are given by natural law? For example, Christ told his followers to turn the other cheek when abused, whereas the natural law suggests that everyone has a right to self-defence and self-preservation.
- Finally, and more generally, we need to ask if people are in fact motivated by reason. One could argue that most moral choices are made as the result of unconscious promptings that are based on needs laid down in infancy, rather than a logical assessment of the final goal of human life.

Natural law shows what our moral life should be like, on the assumption that we are rational beings and that we live in a world that has been designed by a rational and purposeful creator. If either of these assumptions is challenged, so is the theory of natural law.

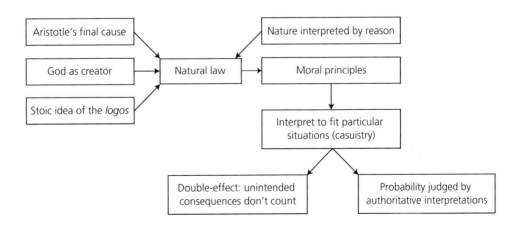

Study guide

By the end of this chapter, you should have considered the view of the universe upon which the natural law approach to ethics is based, and have assessed whether or not you agree that it provides a valid basis for moral decision-making. You should also have taken into account issues connected with any ethical theory that starts with universal principles and applies them to individual situations.

Revision checklist ✓

Can you explain...?

- The difference between an 'efficient cause' and a 'final cause'.
- What is meant by the law of 'double-effect'.
- What is meant by casuistry, and why it is sometimes used in a pejorative sense.

Do you know...?

- Why some Christians might reject the idea of natural law ethics.
- How the natural law theory of Aquinas differed from that of the Stoics. What extra did he bring to that theory?

Give arguments for and against...

- The natural law view that contraception is immoral.

Examples of essay questions

1. To what extent do you consider the natural law view of ethics to be dependent upon belief in God?

AO1 requires appreciation of whether the universe is a rational and purposive place (as Stoics), or impersonal and dominated by chance (as Epicureans). Higher level AO1 will draw out clearly the fact that natural law is based on the idea of a purposeful creation, and thus, for Christianity, belief in God as creator. Students taking papers in Philosophy of Religion may want to relate this to the cosmological and teleological arguments.

AO2 would show how natural law depends on this sense of rational purpose and direction in the universe, and hence – for some – belief in God. Alternatively, it could be argued that a Stoic approach achieves the same ethical theory without the need for the Christian belief in a personal creator. Higher level AO2 will focus on the fundamental question of whether you can have natural order without a divine creator.

2. 'Any sexual aberration which does not allow a person to find fulfilment in married love or in a balanced life of celibacy proves to be a grave encumbrance to freedom and joy, and troublesome in interpersonal relationships' (Bernard Haring, Medical Ethics, St Paul's Publications, 1972). Explain how such a view might be justified by a natural law argument. Do you agree with Haring's statement that other forms of sexuality are 'troublesome'? Give your reasons.

For AO1, students should point out that the natural law interpretation of sex is based on its 'final cause', namely the production of children. Any form of sexuality that does not have that possibility would therefore be regarded as wrong. Higher level AO1 will make clear any examples they use.

For AO2, students should be aware, in saying whether or not they agree, that this very traditional statement comes from a Catholic theologian, written over 35 years ago. They could then argue whether a 'final cause' approach is the only valid way of assessing the place of sexuality. Higher level AO2 might also question whether celibacy is a 'balanced life' in terms of natural law.

Further question

Assess the strengths and weaknesses of the natural law view of ethics.

8 ON WHAT SHOULD MORALITY BE BASED?

Chapter checklist ✓

In this chapter we shall look at a number of thinkers, writing in the seventeenth and eighteenth centuries, who argued that morality is based on emotion, rather than reason, but that it can be expressed and sustained by means of a contract, drawn up either between the ruler and the ruled, or expressing the general will of the people, for their mutual benefit.

What is the starting point for morality? On what should it be based? So far we have looked at three theories – Plato's knowledge of the 'Form of the Good', Aristotle's idea of 'happiness' (*eudaimonia*) and natural law, as presented by the Stoics and then by Aquinas – all of which are based on reason. For all three, knowledge of fundamental features of the world, or of the essence of what it is to be human, is the starting point for living the good life. But there are other possibilities:

- everyone acts in their own self-interest
- people are motivated by emotion rather than reason
- society itself determines what shall be deemed right or wrong, and establishes it by means of a contract between people.

1 Self-interest?

In Plato's *Republic*, Thrasymachus presents the idea that justice is whatever is in the interests of the stronger. He does not present this as an ideal, but simply an observation of what actually happens in society. Plato, in the person of Socrates, finds this inadequate – and does so because he wants a concept of justice that will allow all sections of society to work together for the common good.

But self-interest persists, and for good reason. There are certain situations in which everyone is justified in acting for themselves.

Key people

Spinoza (1632–77)
held the view that self-interest
was bound to be in line with a
rational consideration of a person's
position, since self-preservation
was the most basic need, and it is
perfectly natural and logical for
every creature to seek its own
advantage.

Thus, according to natural law, one has a right to self-defence if one's life is threatened. In the natural world itself, every species seeks to survive and promote itself – and does whatever it takes to achieve that end. If that is how nature works, should it not also work as a basis for morality? In the capitalist world of business, self-interest (in the sense of promoting one's own company or business in a competitive market) is the order of the day.

The problem with taking unqualified self-interest as the basis for morality is that it tends to be self-defeating in a social context. In a competitive environment there will be losers as well as winners. One might be tempted to go for that if there was a very good chance of winning, but what if one might lose? Might it be better to play safe? A modified approach, therefore, would be one in which everyone recognised that, in a society in which people depend on one another, immediate benefits may need to be shared with others in order to gain in the longer term.

Any selfishness in this is modified by the argument that everyone should be able to seek his or her own advantage, not simply be there to satisfy mine. Such a rational approach to self-interest, however, leads to the idea that one might well benefit by seeking an equal advantage for all. So enlightened self-interest recognises the need to enter into agreements with others for mutual benefit – which leads into the various theories of social contract, to which we now turn.

2 Thomas Hobbes

Key people

Thomas Hobbes (1588–1679)
is best known for his political
philosophy. His *Leviathan* (1651)
argues the benefits of a strong
ruler, and reflects his Royalist
sympathies and his horror at the
chaos of the Civil War in England.
He was also a materialist,
considering everything (including
people) to behave in ways that are
mechanical and predictable.

Hobbes argued that there should be a contract between individuals and their ruler. In such a contract the ruler agrees to protect the natural rights of all the individuals who are within his jurisdiction, to act as an arbiter in disputes, and to frame laws which will enable the contract to take effect. If a ruler fails to do this, he or she has forfeited the right to govern.

Hobbes emphasises the importance of having a ruler with powers to enact the laws, otherwise he fears anarchy – a reasonable fear, given that Hobbes was writing (from the safety of Paris, where he was tutoring the future Charles II) of an England that had been torn apart by Civil War. In return, every citizen who lives in, or passes through, the area ruled under this contract, is considered (simply by being there) to have agreed to abide by its terms. But why should such a contract for mutual security be necessary? Hobbes paints a bleak picture of a state of nature in which everyone is out for his or her own survival, a state which he sees reflected in times of war.

Key thought

This reflects the political debates of the 1640s, since *Leviathan* was published in 1651.

A mountain goat has a natural sense of authority; it stands on a high point and threatens to butt any rival who challenges it! That is how goats maintain social order. Is it necessary for a ruler to have absolute power in order to maintain a stable society?

In such condition, there is no place for industry; because the fruit thereof is uncertain; and consequently no culture of the earth … no arts; no letters; no society; and which is worst of all, continual fear, and danger of violent death; and the life of man, solitary, poor, nasty, brutish, and short.

(*Leviathan*, Chapter 6)

In other words, without binding agreements, supported by force if necessary, life would descend into chaos. And clearly the main reason for accepting the authority of such a contract is fear of the anarchic alternative.

Hobbes argues that people should seek peace whenever possible, but if it cannot be achieved, then they have the right to go to war in order to defend themselves. This leads him to what amounts to a version of the 'golden rule':

From this fundamental law of nature, by which men are commanded to endeavour peace, is derived this second law; that a man be willing, when others are so too… [to] be contented with so much liberty against other men, as he would allow other men against himself.

For our purpose, what we need to notice particularly here is the basis for Hobbes' contract: namely, that human nature is observed to be selfish and human action based on emotion rather than reason. People therefore need to agree together on a form of contract that will give them mutual security, and, once established, such a contract can be imposed by means of force, if necessary. Thus Hobbes sees it necessary to construct a state with absolute powers.

Morality is not established (as for Aristotle or Aquinas) in terms of the appreciation of an overall sense of design and purpose, it is imposed by mutual agreement in order to curb the selfishness of human behaviour in a state of nature.

3 John Locke

Key people

John Locke (1632–1704)
Whereas Hobbes was a Royalist, Locke took the Parliamentarian side in the Civil War. The second of his *Two Treatises of Government* (1690) sets out his form of the social contract, and was hugely influential in the development of democratic government. He was concerned to map the limits of human knowledge and is regarded as the first of the great British empiricist philosophers.

Locke also sought to legitimise the authority of the state. In his *Treatises of Government* (1690) he presented the need for a social contract as the basis of morality and social cohesion. Like Hobbes, he starts from a state of nature, but, unlike Hobbes, he does not see this as a state of natural anarchy. Rather, he sees people as having relations with one other and making claims on one another, but needing to have some authoritative and impartial arbiter to decide between competing interests. He is concerned, for example, to establish the right to private property and to the rewards of one's labour (although accepting that servants create property for their masters). He sees the social contract as the means of establishing that authority, and it is an authority that has the tacit consent of all who live within the area of its jurisdiction (as Hobbes). His contract is agreed and justified on the basis that it offers mutual benefit.

Locke moved beyond Hobbes in one crucial respect, namely that for Hobbes the ruler is responsible for the law. Once the contract is in force, the ruler is required to enact such laws as are necessary. For Locke, the ruler is under the law, and the final authority lies not with any individual, but with the institutions of the state – reflecting, of course, his support for the Parliamentarians of his day. Thus it was Locke rather than Hobbes who set down the principles that have led towards modern democracy.

4 Jean-Jacques Rousseau

Key people

Jean-Jacques Rousseau (1712–78)
A most colourful figure, Rousseau wrote fiction and plays, composed music, and seems to have had a remarkable personal life. Increasingly paranoid, he sought to justify himself in his autobiographical *Confessions*. He claimed to be an innocent, corrupted by society – a claim reflected in his philosophy.

Key quote

'Man was born free, and everywhere he is in chains.'

ROUSSEAU

Rousseau took a more positive view of the natural state. He believed that there are two primitive emotions, one is the impulse to self-preservation and the other is a general repugnance at the suffering of others. He therefore considered suffering and social inequality to be the result of the corruption by society of otherwise naturally good people.

Unlike Hobbes, who thought it necessary that the law should be imposed on people, Rousseau argues that the only authority should be 'the general will'. All citizens freely give up their absolute liberty to do exactly as they wish, in order that everyone may enjoy a basic 'civil liberty'. But the acceptance of law is something that comes from the people, it cannot be imposed on them.

The assumption Rousseau makes here is that the interests of the individual are in line with the interests of the state as a whole, and therefore that the establishing of civil liberties will be to the individual's own benefit. Rousseau sees morality as expressed through the conscience of the individual, but it is always acted out in a social context – moral issues concern the way we treat one another, and the task of a just and moral society is to enable that natural moral sense to be exercised, without placing obstacles in its way.

5 Modern contract and rights-based approaches

Key thought

Social contract ideas were also put forward by Thomas Paine (1737–1809) and J. S. Mill (1806–73), developing the concept of the rights of the individual within a democracy and considering the competing claims of individuals and minorities within society.

Following Hobbes, one can see that, if a group of people gather together and decide on a contract to specify how they should treat one another and what rights are to be allowed to one another, then – once that contract is agreed – everyone should be free from the fear that his or her rights are going to be abused. Thus, even if it would be in the interests of a majority, the rights of the individual should not be set aside. This approach was taken by John Rawls in his important book on political philosophy, *A Theory of Justice* (1971),

Key people

John Rawls (1921–2002)
was an American philosopher who taught for many years at Harvard. He was concerned with the idea of justice as fairness, building on the work of the earlier social contract thinkers outlined in this chapter. His *A Theory of Justice* (1971) has been hugely influential and much debated within political philosophy, with clear implications for ethics as a whole.

where he bases his idea of justice on a thought experiment that takes the form of a social contract.

The people who gather to set down the terms of that contract have to set aside all the particular features that distinguish themselves from others. In other words, they have to forget who they are. Since they do not know their place in society, Rawls argues that they will opt to support the most disadvantaged in society, since they do not know whether or not they themselves will come into that category. Thus they are able to see the justice of providing for others, without any thought that, in order to do so, they themselves might lose out. He argues that each individual should have as much liberty as is consistent with allowing a similar liberty to everyone.

In the sphere of political ethics, rights-based approaches have also been taken by Robert Nozick and Ronald Dworkin. John Mackie and others have suggested that all moral theory should be based on a concept of rights. And of course, the Universal Declaration of Human Rights is an important statement of global morality.

Contract and rights-based approaches are also important in areas of applied ethics. Medical ethics provides an example of both contract-based ethics (since there is an implied contract between doctor and patient), and also an approach in which individual patients are deemed to have rights that need to be protected.

Examples

1 In many situations there is either a literal or an implied contract. If you buy goods from a shop and find they are faulty, you can expect to return them and have them replaced. This is simply because the act of buying and selling involves a contract. To sell faulty goods and then refuse to take responsibility for them is deemed a crime (because the implied contract has been broken). On the other hand, one may be asked to sign a disclaimer to the effect that the seller does not guarantee the quality of what is sold. Cheap second-hand cars, for example, are sometimes 'sold as seen', which means that the contract between buyer and seller is one that recognises the possibility that the car has faults.

2 A person is deemed to have certain rights and if those rights are denied, then they can claim compensation. Thus one can argue for the right to travel freely and to hold a passport. In order to stop you travelling there has to be a good reason to withhold that right (for example, on the

> grounds that you are likely to cause a disturbance at a football match abroad). People sometimes claim the right to be able to parade or hold a political rally in areas where that is likely to cause disturbance. In such cases, respect for that right is balanced against the anticipated results of exercising it, for example, if a riot might break out.

The details of the work of all the thinkers mentioned so far in this chapter is a matter of politics rather than ethics. As far as ethical theory is concerned, all we need to note is that justice and morality are regarded as enshrined within a mutual agreement, and implemented by common consent through the institutions of the state. The contract is judged according to whether or not it can deliver individual rights and freedoms compatible with the welfare of the whole of society. For practical purposes, morality becomes a human construct, necessitated either in order to overcome natural aggression or to enhance the natural desire for co-operation.

6 Emotions?

Thomas Hobbes believed that morality was a matter of the passions:

All voluntary motions are preceded by thought, planning out the action for a purpose. That depends on appetite or desire. Love or hate, appetites and aversions are the source of thoughts leading to voluntary actions.

And such emotions lead people to call one thing good and another bad:

But whatsoever is the object of any man's appetite or desire, that is it which he for his part calleth good: and the object of his hate and aversion, evil; and of his contempt, vile and inconsiderable. For these words of good, evil, and contemptible, are ever used with relation to the person that useth them: there being nothing simply and absolutely so; nor any common rule of good and evil, to be taken from the nature of the objects themselves; but from the person of the man, where there is no commonwealth; or, in a commonwealth, from the person that representeth it; or from an arbitrator or judge, whom men disagreeing shall by consent set up, and make his sentence the rule thereof.

(*Leviathan*, Chapter 6)

Key thought

In other words, nothing is 'good' in itself, but it is only called good because it is desired, but there may be a common agreement between people about what they will consider good.

Key people

David Hume (1711–76)
was a key figure in the Scottish Enlightenment, and was both a philosopher and a historian. As an empiricist, he saw all knowledge as based on reason and evidence, and was critical of the idea of miracles and of the design argument for the existence of God. In ethics, however, he recognised the limitations of reason and argued that the emotions were the starting point for moral judgements.

Key quotes

'The same motives always produce the same actions: The same events follow from the same causes. Ambition, avarice, self-love, vanity, friendship, generosity, public spirit; these passions, mixed in various degrees, and distributed through society, have been, from the beginning of the world, and still are, the source of all the actions and enterprises, which have ever been observed among mankind.'

HUME, *AN ENQUIRY CONCERNING HUMAN UNDERSTANDING*

'Reason is, and ought only to be the slave of the passions, and can never pretend to any other office than to serve and obey them.'

HUME, *A TREATISE ON HUMAN NATURE*, 1739–1740

Key people

Francis Hutcheson (1694–1746)
was an Irish philosopher who taught at Glasgow University. Arguing that feelings were the starting point for morality, he anticipated the twentieth-century 'emotivist' approach to ethics.

Notice however that Hobbes, like the utilitarians we shall be considering in the next chapter, was quite prepared to accept that we act on the basis of anticipated results. As we deliberate about what to do:

> *… the appetites and aversions are raised by foresight of the good and evil consequences, and sequels of the action whereof we deliberate; the good or evil effect thereof dependeth on the foresight of a long chain of consequences of which very seldom any man is able to see to the end. But so far as a man seeth, if the good in those consequences be greater than the evil, the whole chain is that which writers call* apparent *or* seeming good.

In other words, we act on emotion, but also seek to assess results. In the end, however, such assessment is never exhaustive, and so we settle for whatever seems to us to offer the best balance in favour of the good.

Locke argued that 'good' is whatever increases pleasure and diminishes pain, but his pupil, the third Earl of Shaftesbury (1671–1713), went on from this to say that moral judgements follow a moral sense of what is amiable, and thus are based on emotion rather than reason. He introduced what became known as the 'moral sense' basis for ethics. He argued also that a virtuous man was one who regulated his inclinations and affections in such a way as to allow them to become harmonious with the inclinations and affections of other people.

The major issue here (as with Hume later) will be how moral sense is related to reason. Certainly for Locke, humankind is driven by its passions. Reason plays a secondary role in assessing what should be done, but does not initiate action. This is also the position of Shaftesbury, since the pleasure we find in thinking about virtue stems from our natural altruism. Notice how the assessment of emotion is quite different in Shaftesbury and Hobbes: for the former we are naturally altruistic, for the latter, naturally selfish.

Hutcheson continued this 'moral sense' tradition, taking the view that there was a natural sense of benevolence, and everyone fundamentally wished the welfare of everyone else. It was Hutcheson who first produced the idea that was to be the basis of utilitarianism:

> *… that nation is best which produces the greatest happiness for the greatest numbers, and that worst which in like manner occasions misery.*
>
> (*An Enquiry into the Original of our Ideas of Beauty and Virtue*, 1725)

It is important to recognise that this utilitarian view works because benevolence is assumed, and therefore the issue of 'Why should I want the greatest happiness for the greatest number?' does not arise.

Bishop Butler put forward the view (in his *Fifteen Sermons*, 1726) that everyone has a 'superior principle of reflection or conscience' and that this 'distinguishes between the internal principles of the hearts, as well as his external actions'. In other words, conscience is brought to bear in trying to balance duty and happiness, although Butler is forced to admit that these two things do not always coincide. The important contribution of Butler here is the idea of a hierarchy of principles, which defines human nature and which assesses and directs the actions which we take in response to the natural promptings of our emotions (see also page 145).

Key thought

Notice in all this how important the individual has become. With the rise of Protestantism and the Civil War, people are more aware of themselves and their inclinations, recognising the need for individuals to contract together for mutual benefit. We are entering a world where morality is linked to democracy, where enlightened self-interest determines that individuals need to accept some curbing of their natural inclinations for the common good, and (for those taking a more positive view of human nature) where the natural inclination to help those in need finds expression.

Key quote

'[It] cannot be disputed, that there is some benevolence, however small, infused into our bosom; some spark of friendship for human kind… Let these generous sentiments be supposed ever so weak… where everything else is equal, [they] produce a cool preference of what is useful and serviceable to mankind, above what is pernicious and dangerous.'
HUME, *AN ENQUIRY CONCERNING THE PRINCIPLES OF MORALS*, 1751

Hume clarified the relationship between emotion and reason in this way – that the passions are what motivate us to act, and that we all have a natural capacity to sympathise with the sufferings of others and to want to help them. But once that emotional motivation suggests a course of action, reason steps in and informs the passions about their effectiveness in terms of gaining happiness from the actions that they propose. In other words you have an emotional impetus that is assisted by reason, in deciding what is right.

In seeing morality as based on the passions, he also pointed out that you could not derive an 'ought' from an 'is' (see page 30) and thus that no amount of argument based on facts about the world would be sufficient to establish a moral law. He accepted the long-term benefit of establishing and obeying rules, because we all have needs and desires, and if those desires are served best by keeping rules, then we ought to do so. In other words, obedience is in line with self-interest.

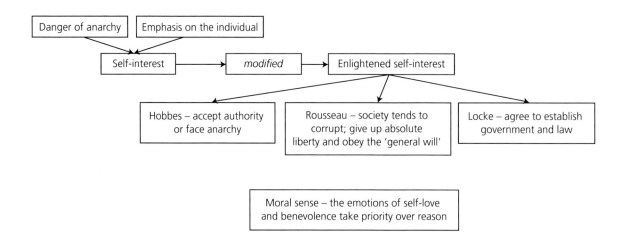

Study guide

By the end of this chapter you should have an appreciation of the 'social contract' approach to ethics, and the fact that from the eighteenth century there was more of an emphasis on the individual. There was also the 'moral sense' approach to ethics, namely that we all have a natural benevolence towards others, as well as self-love, and it is this that prompts moral consideration of how we behave.

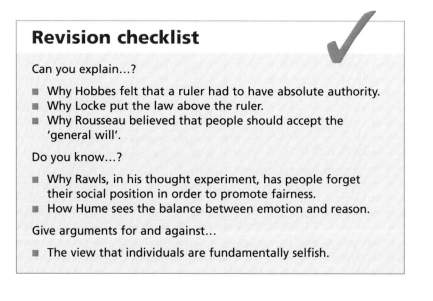

Revision checklist

Can you explain...?

■ Why Hobbes felt that a ruler had to have absolute authority.
■ Why Locke put the law above the ruler.
■ Why Rousseau believed that people should accept the 'general will'.

Do you know...?

■ Why Rawls, in his thought experiment, has people forget their social position in order to promote fairness.
■ How Hume sees the balance between emotion and reason.

Give arguments for and against...

■ The view that individuals are fundamentally selfish.

Examples of essay questions

1. Hobbes takes a negative view of humankind in its natural state, whereas Rousseau takes a positive one. How does their view of the natural state influence their ethics? Which of these do you believe to be the more realistic?

AO1 would include the way in which Hobbes' ethics reflects the fear of anarchy and therefore the need for the security of a strong and absolute ruler. Rousseau's more positive view allows him to see a benevolent role for the 'general will' which, once expressed, commands the loyalty of individual citizens.

AO2 invites a choice of the more positive or negative views of humankind, with reasons and, perhaps, examples. In assessing whether or not these views are realistic, you could also explore whether ethics based on a contract will achieve anything. In other words, if humankind's natural state is a destructive one, can any contractual agreement overcome it? On the other hand, if people are naturally altruistic and friendly, are such agreements necessary at all?

2. Rawls creates a hypothetical situation in which people draw up the rules for their society whilst forgetting who they are, thereby always favouring those least privileged. Do you think this is a realistic approach? To what extent are factional interests a natural and necessary part of society?

For AO1, this question requires a basic knowledge of the positions taken by Rawls.

For AO2, this question gives an opportunity to explore whether, given the chance, one would opt for a 'safe' approach and legislate to support the weak, or take a risk of promoting a more competitive society. Is enlightened self-interest the only basis on which people negotiate agreements? You might approach it by discussing the validity of using 'thought experiments' like these in philosophy.

Further questions

1 Is civil disobedience or the deliberate overthrowing of an elected government ever justified? At what point, if at all, would you consider that a government had lost its right to govern?

2 Are people fundamentally motivated to act by their emotions and, if so, are those emotions, on balance, naturally more selfish or more altruistic?

9 UTILITARIANISM

Chapter checklist

In this chapter we shall examine the principle forms of utilitarianism, along with criticisms of this approach.

Key word

Utilitarianism: an ethical theory by which actions are judged according to their anticipated benefits to the people involved.

Utilitarianism has been one of the most widespread and influential ethical theories. In its simplest form it is based on the 'principle of utility' which is that, in any situation where there is a moral choice, one should do that which results in the greatest happiness for the greatest number of people (a phrase apparently coined by Frances Hutcheson, see page 78). The theory of utilitarianism was set out by Bentham and developed by J. S. Mill and later by Sidgwick and it continues to command the attention of philosophers, notably Peter Singer.

1 Jeremy Bentham

Key people

Jeremy Bentham (1748–1832) was much concerned with the social conditions of his day, with injustice, and with a failure of the law to defend the poorest in society. He was particularly involved both with hospitals and prisons. He sought a moral theory in which whatever was done in a society would be judged to be right or wrong according to whether or not it benefited a majority of those involved, not just a wealthy or privileged minority.

Bentham argued for the 'principle of utility', by which an action is judged good or bad according to the results that it achieves.

> *By utility is meant that property of any object, whereby it tends to produce benefit, advantage, pleasure, good, or happiness, (all this in the present case comes to the same thing) or (what comes again to the same thing) to prevent the happening of mischief, pain, evil, or unhappiness to the party whose interest is considered: if that party be the community in general, the happiness of the community: if a particular individual, then the happiness of that individual.*
>
> (*An Introduction to the Principles of Morals and Legislation*, 1789, Chapter 1, section 3)

Bentham worked on the assumption that society is a collection of individuals, and that what is right for society depends on securing the happiness of those individuals. In his assessment, he wanted everyone to count equally, since he believed that everyone had an equal right to happiness, irrespective of their situation. He suggested that happiness, or benefit, should be measured in terms of:

- its duration
- its intensity
- how near, immediate and certain it is
- how free from pain, and whether or not it is likely to lead on to further pleasure.

Each action, for Bentham, is thus good or bad according to its predicted results in generating the maximum amount of happiness, shared between the maximum number of people involved. His assessment was therefore essentially quantitative, and it was made on the basis of individual actions. Whether or not an action also conformed to a rule or law was a matter of secondary consideration – his primary interest was with the benefits generated and how they were shared. Bentham also took the view that acting according to this principle would itself bring about an individual's greatest happiness. The principle of utility could therefore be followed for the pleasure of doing so, quite apart from the benefit it offered others.

Key words

Consequentialism: used of any ethical theory that considers the consequences of an action. Hence, utilitarianism is one form of consequentialism.

Hedonic calculus: refers to the process (as exemplified by Bentham) of attempting to calculate the benefit or harm caused by an act.

2 John Stuart Mill

Key people

John Stuart Mill (1806–73) was educated at home and precociously intellectual in his youth. He worked as an editor and in business before becoming involved with politics as MP for Westminster. He argued for women's rights, for utilitarian ethics and particularly for individual freedom. His best known works are *Utilitarianism* and *On Liberty*.

Key quote

'Men lose their high aspirations as they lose their intellectual tastes, because they have not time or opportunity for indulging them; and they addict themselves to inferior pleasures, not because they deliberately prefer them, but because they are either the only ones to which they have access or the only ones which they are any longer capable of enjoying.'

MILL, *UTILITARIANISM*

There are many forms of benefit or happiness, and Mill argued that they should not all be considered to be of equal value. He therefore wanted to go beyond the quantitative assessment of benefits offered by Bentham, and to offer an assessment of benefits that would place greater emphasis on what he considered the 'higher pleasures'. He was, however, quite realistic about human nature in this respect:

> *It may be objected that many who are capable of the higher pleasures occasionally, under the influence of temptation, postpone them to the lower… They pursue sensual indulgences to the injury of health, though perfectly aware that health is the greater good… Capacity for the nobler feelings is in most natures a very tender plant, easily killed, not only by hostile influences, but by mere want of sustenance; and in the majority of young persons it speedily dies away in the occupations to which their position in life has devoted them, and the society into which it has thrown them, are not favourable to keeping that higher capacity in exercise.*
>
> (*Utilitarianism*, Chapter 2)

Key thought

SELF-SACRIFICE

A possible objection to utilitarian arguments is that, in calculating the happiness to be achieved, they do not appreciate the value of self-sacrifice, which features highly in traditional Christian morality. Mill has two things to say to counter this. The first is to link his theory with Jesus' teachings, by claiming that to love your neighbour as yourself constitutes 'the ideal perfection of utilitarian morality'. The second is to give a positive role for self-sacrifice:

'The utilitarian morality does recognise in human beings the power of sacrificing their own greatest good for the good of others. It only refuses to admit that the sacrifice is itself a good. A sacrifice which does not increase or tend to increase the sum total of happiness, it considers as wasted.'

Utilitarianism, 1863, Chapter 2

Key word

Rule utilitarianism: utilitarian theory that takes into account the benefits gained by obeying general rules of conduct.

Key thought

The distinction is sometimes made between *strong* rule utilitarianism and *weak* rule utilitarianism, the former holding that one should never break a rule that is established on utilitarian principles, the latter holding that there may be situations when the likely outcome of a particular act may take precedence over the general rule in a utilitarian assessment, although of course that rule still needs to be taken into account.

Key word

Act utilitarianism: utilitarian theory applied to individual actions.

Mill also went beyond Bentham in proposing a positive place for rules within an overall utilitarian approach. The example he uses is of a person who tells a lie in order to get some immediate advantage. He argues that society needs the principle of truthfulness, without which nobody would ever be able to trust anybody to be telling the truth. Therefore, the rule that one should tell the truth is a general means of securing the greatest happiness for the greatest number. Breaking that rule, although it might appear to offer greater happiness in the immediate situation, will in the long run lead to less happiness. Hence he accepts what we term '**rule utilitarianism**'.

Mill gives two examples of situations where he considers that it would be right not to tell the truth:

- One should not give information to someone who is likely to use it to further an evil purpose.
- One should withhold bad news from someone who is dangerously ill, for fear of causing him or her harm.

These show that Mill is still prepared to consider the direct results of individual actions as well as the rules that are thought to offer general good to society. It is also worth noting that, for Mill, the ultimate justification for moral choice, and for utilitarian and all other forms of morality, is 'the conscientious feelings of mankind'. Thus, although we appear to have in utilitarianism an almost mechanical way of gaining an objective assessment of what is right or wrong (by setting out the predicted results of an action), in the end, even the application of that principle is based on a fundamental moral sense that people have.

Some modern approaches to **act utilitarianism** tend to say that an act should be considered good if, on balance, it produces enough happiness, rather than requiring it to produce the maximum possible happiness. This is part of a general attempt to make utilitarian theories workable in practice, without making demands for certainty (either in terms of assessing all the possible future consequences of an action, or checking the consequences of each alternative course of action) that are impossible to satisfy.

Mill himself – in *On Liberty* – set a clear limit to what an individual should be free to do, namely that his or her action should not harm others. Provided it concerns only that individual, there should be complete freedom. Notice that this sets clear limits to those things about which a utilitarian ethic can comment. Natural law claimed that it was able to comment on the rightness or wrongness of actions that concerned only the individual (solitary masturbation, for example), whereas Mill's position would suggest that such things are a matter of personal preference and freedom.

3 Preference and motive utilitarianism

Key word

Preference utilitarianism: utilitarian theory that takes into account the preferences of all those involved in a particular course of action.

So far, in considering Bentham and Mill, we have examined 'act' and 'rule' utilitarianism, but alongside the assessment of acts and of those rules that are deemed overall to benefit society, there are other factors that may be taken into account in a utilitarian assessment: the preferences of those involved, and the motives for acting in a particular way.

In his book *The Language of Morals* (OUP, 1973) R. M. Hare not only set out the basis of a prescriptivist approach to moral language (see above page 41) but also argued for what may be termed **preference utilitarianism**. In this, the utilitarian assessment of a situation takes into account the preferences of the individuals involved, except where those preferences come into direct conflict with the preferences of others. So the right thing to do in any situation is to maximise the satisfaction of the preferences of all those involved. This gets round the problem of using utilitarianism to impose one idea of happiness on someone who might have a very different one. On the other hand, what I prefer to do may not coincide with what is in my own interest. Hence, it may be necessary to distinguish between 'preference utilitarianism' and 'interest utilitarianism'.

There has always been a problem for utilitarianism in terms of an assessment of the motive a person may have for carrying out an action. Can something be right on utilitarian principles even if the motive for doing it is wrong? This question was addressed by Henry Sidgwick (1838–1900), who came to the view that the *outcome* of an action, in terms of the happiness it causes, need not

Key question

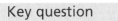

Does this give us a way of judging one motive to be better than another?

Key question

A capitalist buys and improves a company to the benefit of all involved. If his or her motivation was greed and personal gain, does that make such greed good?

Key quote

'[If]… general happiness will be more satisfactorily attained if men frequently act from other motives than pure universal philanthropy, it is obvious that these other motives are reasonably to be preferred on Utilitarian principles.'

SIDGWICK, THE METHODS OF ETHICS, 1874

be what actually *motivates* that action, nor need it be necessarily the *best* motive for that action.

Bentham argued that a person's motive on any given occasion may be judged better or worse depending on the utility of having that motive on that occasion. In other words, the motive itself is considered good if, as a result of having it, happiness is to be increased. But that does not seem to imply – as Sidgwick later pointed out – that the motive itself has to be the desire for the greatest happiness of the greatest number.

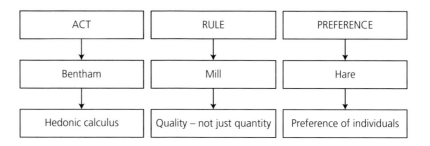

4 Utilitarianism in practice

Key people

Peter Singer (b.1946)
is one of the best-known and often controversial utilitarian thinkers today. Taking a preference utilitarian approach, he tackles key issues, including abortion and euthanasia. He is particularly well known for his work on the ethics of the treatment of other species. Just as those who take a narrow view on race or sex are seen as 'racist' or 'sexist', he argued (in *Animal Liberation*, 1976) that those who fail to do justice to the rights of animals are 'speciesist'.

Take the example of a doctor who is called to the scene of an accident and is required to re-set a broken bone and perform other emergency procedures. His action is almost certain to cause additional pain to those injured. Is that pain good or bad? The answer here seems clear enough, since short-term pain is outweighed by the long-term good of having limbs that grow straight. If you cause pain in the process of saving a life, there seems to be no doubt that, based on a utilitarian assessment of results, that action can be judged good.

Similarly, given the possibility of sharing happiness widely or offering it to a minority at the expense of a majority, it seems fairly clear (and certainly would have been so to those who sought social reform in the eighteenth and nineteenth centuries) that the former is the 'right' thing to do.

On the other hand, in using this argument, we need a fairly clear idea of what constitutes 'happiness'. In other words, as it is put into practice, utilitarianism requires:

- some overall set of values by which to assess happiness
- the ability to predict which course of action is most likely to secure that happiness.

Utilitarian considerations are applied to a wide range of problems within applied ethics. Medical experimentation, whether on animals

Key thought

Such prediction is always going to be provisional. It is always possible to revise one's estimate of long-term harm or benefit.

or humans, for example, is justified in terms of the anticipated benefit to other people that may result from an advance in knowledge. In environmental debates, whether it is the preservation of the environment or the protecting of rare species, the argument used is often utilitarian – that everyone will benefit in the long run from present restraint or intervention.

In the practical application of utilitarianism, it is crucial to be aware of the presuppositions of those who assess what may be considered the 'happiness' or 'benefit' that is to be maximised, and where this is lacking, utilitarian arguments on their own are not persuasive. It may be true that, by taking a certain course of action, more people will live longer. But does that constitute the greatest happiness to the greatest number? There are many other factors to be considered.

5 Criticisms of utilitarianism

The danger of a utilitarian quest to distribute benefits equally is that it may lead to dull uniformity. Preference utilitarianism tries to overcome this. But what if everyone would prefer to live in a house but population density and the economy determine that cheap, high-rise flats are the only option? Do utilitarian arguments simply mask real-world determinism?

One can argue that the concept of happiness is so broad that it can be taken as the name for whatever a person takes as his or her personal goal. If that were to be the case, then, from the standpoint of the agent, utilitarianism offers no objective method of assessing the rights or wrongs of an action. Other people, with different concepts of happiness, will come to different assessments. In such a situation, without an agreed definition of what constitutes happiness, nothing much has been achieved.

One could go on to say that happiness depends on a framework of values, and therefore that utilitarianism does not provide an independent moral theory, but a mechanical way of assessing the likelihood of achieving already stated personal and moral goals. In the end, utilitarianism must rest on something else.

Example

Imagine a society of sadists applying utilitarian principles to their particular form of pleasure. Inflicting pain would be justified in terms of the resulting happiness. If you then step outside that society and say (taking a strong rule–utilitarian approach) that inflicting pain is wrong because, in the world at large, it causes suffering rather than happiness, the weak utilitarian will object that in this particular situation the immediate satisfaction obtained takes precedence over a rule that does not hold for the people concerned. The preference utilitarian also claims that the sadistic preferences of the agents should be taken into account. In the end, what you seem to have is a form of 'social contract' based on the passions, but not an independent or objective way of determining whether sadism is right or wrong.

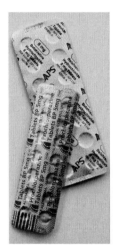

Drugs and treatment cost money. How should a health service with limited funds allocate them?

The validity of using the mechanism of utilitarianism seems obvious in some cases, but not in others. Take the example of the availability of expensive medical treatment in a situation where funding is limited. For the price of one major operation, many other people's lives could be benefited or even saved by more cost-effective remedies. Does that mean that it would be wrong to operate? Or consider the situation where, as a result of the plight of an individual becoming known, many people generously contribute funds to enable that person to have specialist treatment. On a utilitarian assessment that is still a good thing, since the many who contribute do so voluntarily and therefore gain happiness in doing so.

But notice how curious this conclusion is, for the same thing can be considered wrong if imposed on people (forcing everyone to contribute for the benefit of an individual) but right if done voluntarily. This does not sound much like an objective way of assessing right and wrong, merely a way of assessing its social acceptability – which is why Hare and others have sought to take into account both preferences and motives.

Not all are satisfied with a broadly utilitarian approach to medical issues. In her book *The Elimination of Morality* (Routledge, 1993), Anne Maclean criticises Peter Singer and others for what she sees as the removal of all moral concepts that cannot be justified on strictly utilitarian terms. Indeed, she is critical of the whole area of philosophy and bio-ethics. She does not want to deny that there can be rational answers to moral questions, but she opposes the idea that 'for any moral question, there is a *uniquely* rational answer to it which can be uncovered by philosophical enquiry.' (op. cit. page 5). In other words, utilitarianism should not be presented as the *only* way to assess right and wrong.

Another criticism is that utilitarianism does not seem to account for those situations where a person feels that there is something they should do, irrespective of the consequences. It was pointed out above that Mill accepted the notion of self-sacrifice, but that he considered it wasted unless the sum of human happiness was increased as a result.

What of situations where a person dies in a failed attempt to save the life of another? According to Mill's argument, that act of self-sacrifice is wasted, since as a result of it two people are dead

Key thought

For utilitarianism, *goodness does not inhere in an action*, but is only given by setting that action in the context of the greatest happiness for the greatest number.

rather than one. But is there not a sense that the act of trying to save the life of another human being, however unlikely it is to succeed, is not in some way inherently good? This is not to say that a utilitarian could find no way of justifying such an action – it could, for example, be an inspiration to many others – but it seems curious that the inherent value of that action depends on such results.

One of the most succinct and pertinent challenges to the utilitarianism of Mill was presented by G. E. Moore in his *Principia Ethica* (1903). In that book he is concerned to refute the 'naturalistic fallacy' – namely the attempt to derive an 'ought' from an 'is'. He sees this as a feature of almost all previous moral systems (only Plato and Sidgwick escape his criticism). His criticism is based on his claim that Mill identifies 'good' with 'desirable':

> *The fact is that 'desirable' does not mean 'able to be desired' as 'visible' means 'able to be seen'. The desirable means simply what* ought *to be desired or* deserves *to be desired… 'Desirable' does indeed mean 'what it is good to desire'; but when this is understood, it is no longer plausible to say that our only test of that, is what is actually desired. Is it merely a tautology when the Prayer Book talks of* good *desires? Are not* bad *desires also possible?*

In other words, Moore accuses Mill of slipping in an 'ought' where he should be speaking about what 'is', as a matter of fact, desired. Notice that this criticism could apply equally to Bentham, who opens his exposition of utilitarianism by saying that the sovereign powers of pain and pleasure should determine what we ought to do, as well as what we in fact do.

Bernard Williams ('A Critique of Utilitarianism' in *Utilitarianism: For and Against* by J. J. C. Smart and Bernard Williams) has argued that a person's moral identity is rooted in his or her personal commitments. In other words, the basis of morality is in personal values and projects – these constitute what the person stands for, and given a situation of moral choice, they are the things likely to decide what action should be taken.

By contrast, utilitarianism, because it requires an 'objective' assessment of results in order to justify a moral decision, requires a person to set aside personal values and commitments, and start again with each new decision. Williams wants to re-instate a place for personal integrity, which – on purely utilitarian terms – is 'more or less unintelligible'. In practice, one therefore has to ask if a commitment-less approach is realistic, or indeed if it is the way in which people actually make moral decisions. *Williams has argued that we therefore need a more agent-centred approach.*

Another line of criticism, presented by John Rawls, is that utilitarianism does not take seriously the distinction between

Key people

Bernard Williams (1929–2003) was a Cambridge philosopher particularly concerned to reinstate the importance of personal motivation and emotion in ethical discussion. He wanted to move ethical discussions away from narrow ideas of moral obligation to a broader concept of what it meant to live a good life, criticising both utilitarianism and Kantian ethics for claiming to offer universally applicable theories.

persons. This approach considers that utilitarian arguments can too easily be used to justify an impersonal approach, so that the rights of individuals are set aside for some greater good. It would also justify a paternalistic approach whereby the state could decide that your own happiness could be enhanced by measures which you personally would not wish to accept. Like Bernard Williams' approach, the key feature here is the recognition of individuals and their rights, integrity, preferences and personal projects. These things, it is argued, show the inadequacy of any moral system which is based on some general or impersonal assessment.

A more general problem with any form of utilitarianism is the inability ever to achieve a definite assessment of the total of happiness or suffering achieved by any action. This problem had been anticipated by Hume. *The effects of an action form part of a chain that stretches into an indefinite future. There is always the possibility that a very positive result of an action may subsequently lead to very negative consequences.*

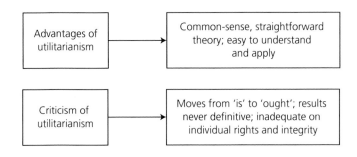

Study guide

By the end of this chapter you should have a basic understanding of the three main forms of utilitarianism – act, rule and preference – and be able to assess their strengths and weaknesses.

Revision checklist ✔

Can you explain...?

- What is meant by the 'principle of utility'.
- How Mill's utilitarianism differed from that of Bentham.
- How Sidgwick relates motives to outcomes.

Do you know...?

- Why one might prefer preference utilitarianism to the earlier versions.
- Why Moore accused utilitarianism of the 'naturalistic fallacy'.

Give arguments for and against...

- The strong utilitarian view that it is never right to break a rule that has been established on utilitarian principles.

Revision exercise

Choose a moral issue (e.g. capital punishment; the lowering of the age of consent for homosexuals; sex outside marriage) and show how you would approach it from the standpoints of act utilitarianism, rule utilitarianism and preference utilitarianism. Then say which of these you find most helpful as a basis for an ethical argument, giving your reasons.

Examples of essay questions

1. Can self-sacrifice ever be right? Discuss with reference to utilitarian views of morality.

AO1 here would require an outline of the utilitarian approach, that is that it depends on results, along with an argument about the actual or intended results of self-sacrifice. Higher level AO1 might give at least one example to make clear.

For AO2, a discussion of this should consider whether or not results give a fair indication of the moral value of an action in such a case. This could range from the 'you can never fully know...' view of results to an argument that results are not relevant to some moral actions.

2. If utilitarianism depends on assessing the results of an action, can we ever say for certain that something is good or bad? Does this invalidate it as an ethical theory?

AO1 would require an outline of the way in which utilitarianism depends on an assessment of results, and of the difficulty of knowing when to say that all the results are known.

AO2 would require a general assessment of the validity of any consequentialist ethic (i.e. based on results) as opposed to a natural law or Kantian ethic.

3. Should personal commitments take priority over the assessment of the anticipated results of an action? Discuss with reference to Bernard Williams' criticism of utilitarianism.

AO1 would require some appreciation of Williams' views on the ethical significance of personal values and commitments.

AO2 would go on to consider whether these views are correct, and – if so – whether they represent a valid criticism of utilitarianism.

In all these questions on utilitarianism, it is valuable to be able to give examples of the problem of assessing results. Medical ethics provides a whole range of problems of this sort, especially in terms of the allocation of medical resources, as do issues connected with the environment. Since utilitarianism is so widespread, and so often regarded as *the* common-sense, if not the *only* reasonable approach to ethical issues, it is really important to be able to stand back and take a carefully reasoned and critical approach to what it can achieve.

Further questions

1 Does utilitarianism offer values, or merely a mechanism for applying values we already hold?

2 Is utilitarianism consistent with the ethics of the religion you have studied?

Chapter checklist

In this chapter we shall examine Kant's view that ethics can be based on the pure practical reason, with principles that may be applied universally.

Key word

Deontological ethics: a term used for ethical theories that are concerned with 'duties' and with what is 'right' irrespective of any expected results of actions (in contrast to consequentialist theories, such as utilitarianism). Kant's theory is deontological, since it starts with the experience of a moral 'ought' and examines the rational principles that define what is morally right.

Aquinas' sense of natural law, the utilitarian's weighing of the expected results of an action, and considering the obligations of an implied contract and agreement made between people, all attempted to establish some objective basis for moral claims. Immanuel Kant started from a totally different position. He argued that we all know what it is to have a sense of moral obligation – to believe that there is something we ought to do, irrespective of the consequences it may have for us. Starting from that experience of morality, he believed that it should be possible to give a systematic account of our moral duties and of the principles upon which they are founded, which would be based on pure reason, and would therefore be universal.

1 A sense of moral obligation

Key thought

Kant sought to discover and set out a rational basis for one's sense of duty, and from that to devise principles by which one could distinguish right from wrong.

Kant's moral philosophy is a reflection upon the direct experience of morality:

Two things fill the mind with ever new and increasing admiration and awe the oftener and more steadily we reflect on them: the starry heavens above me and the moral law within me. I do not merely conjecture them and see them as though obscured in darkness or in the transcendent region beyond my horizon: I see them before me, and I associate them directly with the consciousness of my own existence.

(*Critique of Practical Reason*, 1788)

PROFILE

Immanuel Kant (1724–1804)

Kant was born, spent his whole life and died in Konigsberg in East Prussia. His most important works include *The Critique of Pure Reason* (1781), the *Groundwork of the Metaphysics of Morals* (1785), and *Critique of Practical Reason* (1788).

Basically, Kant stands as part of the European Enlightenment, the movement to get beyond authority and superstition and deal with the world on the basis of human reason. He had been influenced by German pietism, the view that religion should be based on personal experience, rather than on study or rational proof.

Disturbed by Hume's scepticism about what we could know as a result of sense experience, his own approach was to start with pure reason. What do we know of ourselves as rational beings? The result, which was set out in the *Critique of Pure Reason*, was what he was to call his Copernican Revolution. It had been assumed that sense experience conformed to external reality, but – just as Copernicus had found that his observations made sense once he had realised that the Earth moved round the Sun rather than the other way round – he argued that we experience the world as we do simply because that is the way our senses function.

The religious implications of his views were controversial. Following publication of *Religion Within the Limits of Reason Alone*, he was forbidden by the university to write any more on matters of religion.

Key thought

We know we are free because we experience moral choice; we do not experience moral choice only after coming to the conclusion that we are free.

In his *Critique of Pure Reason*, Kant had examined the traditional arguments for the existence of God and found them wanting. He had also come to the conclusion that our understanding of the world depends to a large extent upon our own faculties. Space, time and causality are not 'out there' to be discovered, but are ways in which our minds order their experience. Taken together, these had a radical impact on his subsequent thinking. In a universe that lacked theological certainty, and in which – looking up at 'the starry heavens' – he was all too aware of human insignificance, he hoped that reason and the experience of morality would restore a sense of human dignity and worth. His moral theory therefore starts with the phenomenon of 'good will' and celebrates what can be achieved by the application of human reason.

He did not look at the world and ask if freedom and moral choice were possible. Instead, he started with the experience of moral choice, and then sought to find its implications.

Kant saw clearly that, where empirical evidence was concerned, there could be no certainty. He also realised (from reading Hume, see above page 78) that one could never argue logically from an 'is' to an 'ought', for facts show what is, not what ought to be. He therefore wanted to find a new starting point for morality, a starting point that was not dependent on anything as ambiguous as evidence, and found it in the idea of the 'good will'.

2 The 'Good Will'

Key quote

'The autonomy of the will is the sole principle of all moral laws and of the duties conforming to them...'

KANT, *CRITIQUE OF PRACTICAL REASON*, BOOK 1, CHAPTER 1

Kant wanted to place the 'good will' at the very centre of ethics, and in doing so, he was to go beyond anything that had been written before. In many ways, Kant represents a turning point in ethics – after his work, it became impossible to ignore the active role of the person who behaves morally; morality is not to be found 'out there' in evidence we can analyse, nor in results we may try to predict, but only in the exercise of freedom and good will in an action.

a) The will and virtue

The second part of Kant's *Metaphysics of Morals* concerns 'the doctrine of virtue'. He follows Aristotle in seeing virtue as a human excellence. What counts, if a person is to do his or her duty, is not mere obedience, but a good will. Having a good will is an attitude, rather than simply a way of behaving. In choosing to act morally, I am exercising an inner freedom in following a sense of my purpose and destiny, and expressing my will and virtues in an exercise of the pure practical reason.

Kant sees the development of virtues as its own reward, and morality – action springing from the pure practical reason – as the sole means of bringing this about. The intention of his morality is to set aside all ego-centredness, and move towards an unconditional and universal sympathy.

Although he acknowledges evil, Kant does not see it as a separate power influencing one's choices or frustrating the working out of the good. Rather, he sees it as a muting of, or failure to acknowledge and respond to, the moral law. Due to our conditioning or circumstances we may be dominated by ego-centredness, and this means that our moral choices will fail the test of the categorical imperative (see below page 99), since they will be based on self-interest.

Key thought

Notice just how different this is from both the Greek and Medieval thinkers we examined earlier. They assumed that in some way 'good' could be defined with reference to the world, and therefore it was something to be discovered and explored, and in line with which one should direct one's action. This is certainly the case, for example, with Aquinas' view of natural law. It is good for everything to follow its natural purpose and end – doing so constitutes its 'good'. But for Kant, 'good' is related to the will, not in a set of values to be found in the world. *The implication of this is that each individual constructs and takes responsibility for his or her own set of moral values.*

b) The *summum bonum*

For Kant the aim of morality is not to gain happiness, but to be *worthy* of happiness. Indeed, he rather despises the person who gains happiness and fortune in life without deserving it. He sees the 'highest good' (*summum bonum*) as the joining of virtue and happiness. But it is virtue, in doing one's duty, that comes first; happiness is always a bonus that may be added, and it cannot be guaranteed. As we shall see below (page 98), this relates closely to his idea of the 'postulates' of the practical reason.

Key quote

'There is no possibility of thinking of anything at all in the world, or even out of it, which can be regarded as good without qualification, except a good will. Intelligence, wit, judgement, and whatever talents of the mind one might want to name are doubtless in many respects good and desirable, as are such qualities of temperament as courage, resolution, perseverance. But they can also become extremely bad and harmful if the will, which is to make use of these gifts of nature and which in its special constitution is called character, is not good. The same holds with gifts of fortune; power, riches, honour, even health, and that complete well-being and contentment with one's condition which is called happiness make for pride and often hereby even arrogance, unless there is a good will to correct their influence on the mind and herewith also to rectify the whole principle of action and make it universally conformable to its end. The sight of a being who is not graced by any touch of a pure and good will but who yet enjoys an uninterrupted prosperity can never delight a rational and impartial spectator. Thus a good will seems to constitute the indispensable condition of being even worthy of happiness.'
Groundwork for the Metaphysics of Morals, 1785

3 The background to Kant's moral theory

To appreciate Kant's ethical argument, we need to look at it in the context of his philosophy as a whole, and in particular the influences upon him.

Kant was influenced by science and by the gathering and assessment of empirical evidence. Indeed, the impetus behind his 'Copernican revolution' was the attempt to reconcile the ambiguity in empirical evidence (nothing is absolutely certain, we have only degrees of probability) that he found in Hume, with the laws of nature as framed by Newton. How can we achieve certainty from evidence alone? His answer, of course, was that we cannot: any certainty must come from the mind, in actively ordering the evidence of the senses. The world is a rational place, organised in time, space and causality, not because we have sufficient evidence to convince us of that fact, but because it is our minds that perceive it that way. So much for his wondering about the starry heavens, but when it came to the experience of the moral law within him, Kant needed to take an equally bold step.

He was concerned by Hume's argument that one cannot rationally move from an 'is' to an 'ought' (in his *A Treatise on Human Nature*, 1739–40). From it he concluded that morality cannot be based on the evidence of the senses. He was also convinced, however, that people had an inherent sense of right and wrong, and was influenced by Rousseau's positive view of human nature (see page 75). His task, therefore, was to reconcile the experience of moral obligation with empirical scepticism.

Key thought

THE SYNTHETIC 'A PRIORI'

Statements are either 'a priori' (prior to experience) or 'a posteriori' (after and based on experience). Kant also distinguished analytic statements (like tautologies, or mathematics, where their truth is known by definition) and synthetic statements, which are known to be true with reference to empirical evidence.

His response to empirical scepticism was therefore to suggest that moral statements were synthetic a priori. In other words, they did not depend on sense experience, but their meaning was not limited to a definition of terms. One implication of this is that such statements could be denied without any logical contradiction (which would not have been the case if they were analytic).

a) Motives

If you are to consider the pure practical reason, you need to eliminate three other reasons why a person might choose to do something:

Key thought

A discount is always offered for good commercial reasons. But it can be argued that we are all a bit commercial in the way we deal with other people.

- **You might do something because you will immediately or eventually benefit from it.**

  In other words, you might act out of enlightened self-interest, even when you appear to be doing something at your own cost. For example, a shopkeeper may reduce the price of his goods, or offer some special deal for regular customers. On the face of it he is thereby limiting his profit and so appears to be offering something for the benefit of others. On the other hand, it is clear that a person may do that for sound commercial reasons. The customer is being offered something in order that, in the longer term, the shopkeeper may benefit. Kant would hold that such a decision cannot be given moral approval, since it is based on anticipated results, not on pure reason.

- **Equally you may do something out of natural interest.**

  Suppose I am fascinated by anatomy. I might offer to help with some major surgical operation. I may indeed make a difference and help the patient recover. Nevertheless the impetus behind my offer of help is purely selfish. I am doing something which I enjoy, not something that I feel I have a duty to do. Kant was even against making sympathy a basis for moral action (as Hume had argued), since it is possible that we may offer sympathy to someone who does not deserve it.

- **You may do something because someone in authority – either a representative of the law, or of a religion, or some other person in a position of responsibility – may tell you to do it.**

  I want to remain on good terms with that person for a whole variety of reasons, and so I decide to obey. But obedience too, although it may be considered to be a virtue (expressing loyalty), is not exactly the same as making a free moral choice.

Kant eliminates these alternative reasons and then looks to see what is left. What motivates moral action that is neither commanded nor promises rewards nor is inherently pleasurable? In his *Groundwork of the Metaphysics of Morals* he sets out three propositions that fix the boundaries of morality:

Key thought

For Kant, the highest form of morality is to do one's duty against one's own inclinations.

- Your action is moral only if you act from a sense of duty.
- Your action is moral only if you act on the basis of a principle, or maxim.
- It is your duty to act out of reverence for the moral law.

Key question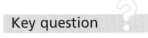

Was Kant a killjoy?

Kant does sound something of a killjoy, since he appears to dismiss action that we find naturally interesting, or to our benefit, or prompted by sympathy or affection. But that is not actually fair to him. He admitted that inclination could still be present (we may, for example, simply enjoy doing our duty) but argued that our inclinations are irrelevant in considering the moral status of our action. In other words, if you enjoy doing something, fine, but don't try claiming that you are being virtuous.

4 The postulates: freedom, God and immortality

Kant argued that, in obeying a moral command, we are accepting three things:

- Freedom – because I experience myself as having a free choice. If it wasn't possible for me to do something, I wouldn't have a sense that I ought to do it.
- God – because if I feel obliged to do something, I must have a sense that the world is designed in such a way that doing the right thing will eventually lead to happiness. In a godless world, nothing would matter.
- Immortality – because I may not be able to achieve the good I seek in following this moral obligation in the course of my lifetime. On the other hand, if I still go ahead and do it, it shows that I am in some way looking beyond this life.

Key thought

Notice that he did *not* mean that we are first convinced of these three things, and then come to the conclusion that it is reasonable therefore to obey any moral command. Rather, that these three things are 'postulates' of the pure practical reason. They are implied in your sense of moral obligation.

Key words

Phenomena: what we experience through the senses.

Noumena: things in themselves, independent of our experience of them.

Key thought

As I am in myself, I am free. As I am observed from the outside, I am conditioned.

In his *Critique of Pure Reason* (1781), Kant distinguished between things as we experience them (which he called **phenomena**) and things as they are in themselves (**noumena**). In the world of phenomena, everything is totally determined, simply because our minds seek reasons for everything that happens. We impose causality upon our experience – it is the only way in which we can make sense of it. So if I look at myself from the outside, as it were, if I turn myself into a *phenomenon*, I shall be totally conditioned. Freedom will vanish, because an omniscient observer would always be able to give reasons why I acted as I did. But Kant holds that we can be *both phenomenally conditioned and noumenally free*.

What Kant is arguing for in *The Critique of Practical Reason* (1788) is the very opposite of what we normally assume in terms of freedom and morality. We would normally examine whether or not we are free, because if we are not then morality makes no sense, since we cannot be praised or blamed for what was beyond our control. Kant, by contrast, points out that the reverse is the case – that it is the experience of the moral law that leads to an awareness of freedom. I only experience freedom when I reflect on the ability I have to make a moral choice.

Thus the immediate awareness of being human entails an awareness of one's own freedom and of the challenge of embodying such freedom in chosen action. Kant's basis for morality is found within our own experience of it.

Key thought

Notice that, for Kant, *acting morally has become an end in itself*, not a means to some other end. Therefore it appears to have certainty in an otherwise uncertain world.

Therefore, according to Kant, one should act as if there were a God, even if God cannot be proved. One acts to fulfil one's own moral imperative as though God had commanded it, without attachment to the results of action. If a person believes in God, behaving morally could be seen as a way to achieve happiness by gaining his approval. On the other hand, Kant wants moral development to be free from all considerations of consequences.

Thinking freedom

We can look at this experience another way. In general, we think of ourselves as individual egos, separated off from one another and from the rest of the world. But as soon as I think of myself in that way, I become part of the phenomenal world; I am an object among other objects, and as such I lose my freedom to act morally, because everything I do is conditioned by what is outside me.

Key thought

What you see is a world where everything is determined by causes; what you feel is the freedom to choose what to do. Morality starts with that feeling of freedom.

But what if I let go of the ego, and therefore drop the distinction between the self and the world? What if I act in a way that is based on pure practical reason, not looking at the possible results of my action? I would be spontaneous, acting solely on the basis of my will, and I would therefore be free.

5 The categorical imperative

Key words

Categorical imperative: a moral 'ought' that does not depend on results.

Hypothetical imperative: something you need to do if you are to achieve a desired result.

We need to distinguish between a **categorical imperative** and a **hypothetical imperative**. A hypothetical imperative tells you what you should do in order to achieve a given result (e.g. if you want to win a race, you will need to train). On the other hand, if you are not interested in the promised result, there is no need to obey the command. All hypothetical imperatives come in the form of an 'if… then' statement. By contrast a categorical imperative tells you that you should do something, without any reference to the likely result (e.g. you should always tell the truth).

Kant's theory of ethics was developed initially in *Groundwork of the Metaphysics of Morals* (1785) and in the *Critique of Practical Reason* (1788). On reflecting on the experience of moral obligation, he found that morality implied a *categorical imperative*, he saw nothing moral in simply following a line of action in order to achieve a desired result. He therefore sought to formulate general rules for testing if something was right or wrong. There are three main forms of the categorical imperative, with a number of different forms of wording, but the first and basic one is:

Key word

Maxim: a principle, or a general rule governing the action of a rational person. It takes the form 'Whenever A happens, I consider it right to do B.'

- So act that the maxim of your will could always hold at the same time as a principle establishing universal law.

This form of the categorical imperative therefore provides a simple, logical test. If you are content that everyone else should be bound by the same principle upon which you are acting, then what you are doing is logically consistent and therefore right. If, on the other hand, what you want to do would involve a contradiction, or be self-defeating, if everyone followed that same **maxim**, then it is wrong.

A stallholder waits for customers. Many social functions invite us to treat people as means to our end (in this case, shopping) rather than ends in themselves. What would it take to treat the stallholder as an 'end' in herself?

Example

Kant illustrated this by considering the situation of someone who needs a loan, and will only get it if he promises to repay it. If he knows that he will not be able to repay it, should he still go ahead and make that promise? Kant argues that it would only be right to make that promise if you could, at the same time, agree that making such a promise (i.e. one you cannot keep) should be made a universal law. But this would involve a contradiction, because promise-making becomes nonsense if everyone is entitled to break their promises. Thus, he reasons, it is always wrong to make a promise which you know you cannot keep.

Notice that the categorical imperative does not tell you the content of your moral obligations. *What it offers is a principle of the pure practical reason – the most general principle possible, namely that something is right only if you can, without contradiction, wish it to become a universal law.*

The second formulation of Kant's categorical imperative concerns the treatment of other people:

- Act in such a way that you always treat humanity, whether in your own person or in the person of any other, never simply as a means, but always at the same time as an end.

This does not mean that a person should never be used as a 'means' – that happens every time we are paid for doing a job of work, for example – but simply that we should, at the same time, be aware of each person as an autonomous agent in his or her own right.

The third form of the categorical imperative highlights Kant's view that it is human reason that determines morality:

- Act as if a legislating member in the universal kingdom of ends.

Key thought

By 'the kingdom of ends' Kant means the society of rational beings, all of whom are to be treated as 'ends' rather than as 'means'.

He argues that we should behave as though we are both members in such a kingdom and also its legislators.

Notice that Kant's morality is a priori. It is established quite apart from a consideration of possible results. In other words, he wants the motive for action to be other than the satisfaction of our immediate sensual desires. This is the very opposite of any form of hedonism or utilitarianism, where the production of happiness is the ground for choice.

Key thought

The implication of Kant's categorical imperative is that, as free, autonomous, rational, moral agents, we do not *discover* morality – we *make* it.

Kant firmly believed that a person experienced his or her own worth primarily when acting in this way, based on a priori reason, and not simply responding to sense experience. Kant's moral vision here is that a person should set aside all narrow considerations of personal gain and have a genuinely universal sympathy. His argument is that, in doing so, one achieves what is highest in human nature.

a) A 'selfish' problem

Kant was trying to express the logical argument that would be presented by someone who was not concerned with his or her own ego, but was genuinely universal in his or her sympathies. To set aside personal consideration is to think universally, and it is therefore reasonable that the maxims of your action should also be universal. The danger with his formulation is that one might use it simply as a basis for calculation from a selfish point of view. For example, I could say that it is wrong to steal, on the grounds that if everyone stole, private property would be in peril and I would have little hope of retaining what I had just stolen. That would be a straight application of the categorical imperative. But I could go on to say that it is wrong to steal except when a person is starving, since I could imagine wanting everyone to be able to steal simply in order to survive – and therefore (since I am starving) it is right for me to steal.

This is an obvious example, but there could be more subtle ones in which the maxim which is to be universalised is so closely defined that it would apply to a very limited number of people, and therefore there would be no contradiction in willing that it should become a universal law. In other words, it would be easy to argue that everyone in exactly the same situation as me should be able to do what I now choose to do, even if everyone in slightly different circumstances is precluded from doing so.

Although that argument is possible, given the logic of Kant's application of the categorical imperative, it is totally against his intention in formulating it – for he wanted to get away from any calculations based on anticipated advantage. He considered the principle of universalisability to be necessary for an action to be considered right: if it cannot be universalised, it can't be right.

b) The problem of others

Kant's moral theory examines what it means to be a free, autonomous, moral legislator. However, in any actual society (as opposed to the ideal 'kingdom of ends') we need to frame moral principles that restrain people from behaving in a way that is destructive of society as a whole. In other words, there will be many practical situations in which we cannot consider everyone as a morally responsible, free and autonomous 'end'. This challenge was raised by Christine Korsgaard in an article in 1986, reproduced in the Sterba anthology (see Further reading).

Kant held that everything either has price or dignity. If it has price, it can be exchanged and replaced by something equivalent. But every human being, as an 'end', is unique and irreplaceable, and therefore has dignity. The problem is how to deal with those who choose to treat other people as though they had price – to treat them as commodities.

Another problem, raised by Alasdair MacIntyre in *After Virtue*, is that Kant's system works on the assumption that everyone is agreed on the final end and purpose of human life. In reality, there is no such agreement. He might want everyone to be free and autonomous; others might not.

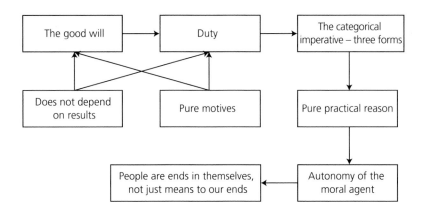

6 Absolute or relative?

Key thought

Axiological ethics is a term sometimes used for the study of the values that underlie the moral choices people make.

Moral choices can be related to the society and particularly to the established values of the society within which they are made. All ethical theories based on contract, for example, carry with them the values of those who enter into that contract.

A key question for ethics is therefore whether all moral issues are culturally conditioned and actions judged right or wrong with reference to the underlying values of society, or whether there is some way of getting beneath the cultural diversity to touch some

Key thought

In the end, Kant's ethical theory comes down to individual integrity. What counts morally is that you should be able to justify what you do rationally and also universalise the maxim that lies behind it.

Key thought

Notice that the key for Kant is *autonomy*. If my intention is right, then I will not act at the whim of my senses, but with autonomy. The principles of my action come from my practical reason alone, they are not imposed on me from outside.

Key question

Kant starts with the experience of moral obligation. But what if people do not feel challenged in this way? What if they claim never to feel they 'ought' to do anything that they do not actually want to do? It is difficult to see how Kant's approach could ever *persuade* someone to act morally. If they already want to do the right thing, Kant's categorical imperative can be used as a guide; but if they do not, Kant would appear to have little to offer.

absolute moral standard. It is this, of course, that Kant attempted to do with the concept of the categorical imperative. It focuses on the sense of moral obligation without reference to the consequences of an action nor yet to the social or cultural matrix of values within which it is experienced.

Just as within his theory of knowledge, Kant saw the mind as having an active role, determining how we are to understand sense perceptions, so in the area of morality the mind is active in pursuit of its highest goals, and only in the light of these does it evaluate sense perceptions in terms of the expected results of action.

But does that provide you with an absolute set of moral values, or one that is relative to its cultural setting? The answer would seem to be that for each individual the moral demand is absolute, in that it is not dependent upon an assessment of facts or predicted consequences. But since no two people will have exactly the same 'good will', and will experience moral demands differently, it means that – in practice – there will be a wide variety of actual ethical practice. Viewed from the outside there will be variety; viewed from the perspective of the moral subject, all may be applying the same principles. In the end, morality depends on values, and it was Kant who recognised that values are something that we impose on experience.

It is difficult to over-emphasise the importance of Kant for the whole development of ethics from his day through to the twenty-first century. *With Kant, the human reason and will stand supreme. Man takes his rational stand and no longer looks outside himself for external guarantors of moral rectitude. God becomes a postulate of pure practical reason, part of the structure within which the mind works.*

It is a short step from this point to start to see the whole of moral value as something that is to be created by the human will and imposed on the external world, or even a philosophy in which human meaning and purpose plays the central role. As we look at Nietzsche, and later at existentialism, we are examining philosophical ideas which look back to the contribution of Kant. His was a Copernican revolution indeed; from then on, all the values are seen as generated by man, not encountered by him.

Key thought

KANT AND DEMOCRACY

Kant's moral theory depends on a kingdom of free, autonomous human beings, each an 'end', each responsible for legislating universally. This was a democratic ideal, from a period that saw both the French and American Revolutions.

Advantages of Kant's approach:
- It conforms to what most people think of as morality.
- It is rational and certain, and does not depend on results or happiness.

Disadvantages of Kant's approach:
- Most people do want to take the result of their actions into account, and may feel guilty if harm comes as a result of their good intentions.
- There is a danger that it will be followed too rigidly. There may be occasions when it would be right to tell a lie, simply because by lying (e.g. to a terrorist about to carry out a bombing) one might achieve a greater good than by conforming to a principle of truth-telling. Kant himself recognised there are situations when circumstances make a general rule inappropriate.
- In a world where everyone is – or wants to be – a rational, autonomous moral agent, Kant's vision of how to decide moral issues could work. It is more problematic when dealing with the more selfish aspects of human nature and the need to control them.

Study guide

By the end of this chapter you should have a clear working knowledge of Kant's moral theory, and particularly of the three forms of the categorical imperative. You should also have a sense of how Kant's moral thinking relates to his theory of knowledge and the role of sense experience.

Revision checklist

Can you explain...?

- What Kant meant by a categorical imperative.
- Why freedom, God and immortality are 'postulates' of the pure practical reason.
- The difference between phenomena and noumena.

Do you know...?

- Why Kant would argue that doing your duty is the only valid motive for morality.
- What Kant meant by a 'synthetic a priori'.

Give arguments for and against...

- The view that it is unrealistic to treat everyone as an 'end' in themselves rather than a 'means'.

Examples of essay questions

1. Explain the difference between a hypothetical and a categorical imperative. Do you think that the categorical imperative, as presented by Kant, provides a sufficient guide to what is right or wrong?

For AO1, one should explain what is meant by the hypothetical and categorical imperative. Higher level AO1 will draw out the actual difference and include at least the first two formulations of the categorical imperative: that one must be able to will that the maxim of your action shall become a universal law, and also that people should be treated as ends and never as means.

For AO2, an evaluation of this would probably best be done via one or two examples of ethical issues. The higher level answers will focus on the key word 'sufficient' – that is whether the categorical imperative alone will show what is right, or whether further consideration needs to be given, as in terms of values held or social conditions.

2. If you do not experience moral obligation, does that imply that nothing you do is right or wrong? Discuss with reference to Kant's ethics.

For AO1, one should explain how Kant's ethics are based on the 'good will' and an experience of a categorical imperative. Higher level answers will establish that Kant's whole rational approach is based on that, making morality dependent upon an individual person's moral and rational sensitivity. Higher level answers might also bring in the three 'postulates' of the practical reason (God, freedom and immortality), which are equally implied by the moral sense, and vulnerable to its absence.

AO2 here would need to show an appreciation of alternative bases for morality – e.g. natural law, utilitarianism or social contract – and comment on whether these are independent of a sense of moral obligation. Higher level candidates might bring in the issue of relativism, which sits uneasily alongside Kantian ethics.

Further questions

1 Kant's ethical theory is based on the autonomy of the moral choice, rather than on the predicted results of an action. Taking as an example one moral issue you have studied, say whether you think Kant's is a suitable starting point for an ethical discussion of that issue, giving your reasons.

2 We discover morality, not make it. Discuss.

11 MORALITY AND POWER

Chapter checklist

In this chapter we shall examine those features of Nietzsche's philosophy that challenged existing ethical theories, in particular the establishment of the future of humankind as a basis for a system of values.

1 Background

Key thought

Nietzsche's view of Christian morality is coloured by this very negative assessment of humankind in its natural state.

Key quotes

'My Ego taught me a new pride, I teach it to men: No longer to bury the head in the sand of heavenly things, but to carry it freely, an earthly head which creates meaning for the earth...
I teach mankind a new will: to desire this path that men have followed blindly, and to call it good and no more to creep aside from it, like the sick and dying...
It is time for man to plant the seed of his highest hope.'

THUS SPOKE ZARATHUSTRA, SECTION 5

In order to appreciate the force of Nietzsche's arguments, one needs to be aware of his background. He was brought up in a religious household (his father was a Lutheran pastor) and he was therefore very familiar with Christian ideas of morality and sin, and was taught that humankind was fundamentally 'fallen'. In other words, in order to receive grace and salvation, a person must first confess that he or she is a sinner, unworthy of God's love. Without God's grace, human beings can achieve nothing.

In terms of philosophy, one can see Nietzsche within a tradition of continental thought that continued Kant's emphasis on the role of the subject self in interpreting and giving structure to the world of experience, and in freely willing and choosing – a tradition which included, for example, Schopenhauer and Fichte.

It is also important to see Nietzsche in the context of the great systems of thought of the nineteenth century – particularly those of Hegel and Marx. Although his approach is very different from theirs, he too thought in terms of an onward process of change. He was also aware of evolution and the newly enhanced view of humankind within the natural order. He did not see humankind as fixed, but in a process of becoming. There is a sense running through many nineteenth-century thinkers that humankind has a destiny waiting to be shaped.

PROFILE

Friedrich Nietzsche (1844–1900)

Friedrich Nietzsche is probably one of the most fascinating and challenging philosophers of modern times. He had the courage to attack key features of the philosophy and religion of his day, and to raise absolutely fundamental questions. His writing is not easy: he distrusted systems of thought, and preferred to hone his insights into short, vivid images. Often his purpose is clearest in his strings of aphorisms (short, pithy statements).

2 God is dead

Key thought

In the opening section of Nietzsche's book *Thus Spoke Zarathustra* (1883–5) the prophet Zarathustra comes down from his mountain retreat and is amazed to find that people are not aware that God is dead.

Key word

Superman: the usual translation of Nietzsche's *Übermensch*, the 'higher man' or 'overman' who would be the next stage in humankind's evolution.

Nietzsche saw the earth as floating free from the constraints of the old theistic structures. The sense of purpose for which Aquinas argued was something that Nietzsche saw as having vanished from the intellectual world of his day. His task, then, is to examine a world without God, and a world within which humankind is at the leading edge of evolution. To do that, he requires two things: courage to face reality, and a desire to establish a new sense of direction now that there is no God to provide it.

The direction Nietzsche finds, in the absence of God, is the next stage in the evolution of humankind, what he terms the 'overman'. If the direction in which humankind is moving is from animal to **Superman**, then this will have profound implications for ethics. Rather than requiring morality to conform to a God-given fixed structure, or a calculation of anticipated benefits, moral assessment is to be made in terms of the direction in which humankind is headed.

3 Willing the Superman

In a marathon, all run together, but each tries to overcome his or her own limitations and to achieve his or her personal goal. Is this a suitable image for Nietzsche's idea of trying to achieve something beyond ourselves? Can we decide a goal that is to be the meaning of the earth for us?

I teach you the Superman. Man is something that should be overcome. What have you done to overcome him?

All creatures hitherto have created something beyond themselves: and do you want to be the ebb of this great tide, and return to the animals rather than overcome man?

The Superman is the meaning of the earth. Let your will say: the Superman shall be the meaning of the earth.

Thus Spoke Zarathustra, section 3

This last statement is crucial for Nietzsche's ethics. Nietzsche sees the will as the point at which morality comes into play. He is asking people to choose – to will – that Superman be the meaning of the earth. It is not a matter of *proving* it to be so, but *willing* it to be so. Once that step is taken, it is important that people should will the future of the earth, and not try to locate their personal goals in

Key quote

'Man is a rope, fastened between animal and Superman – a rope over an abyss.'
THUS SPOKE ZARATHUSTRA, SECTION 4

some heavenly realm. He called those who were concerned mainly with spiritual things and with rewards after death the 'afterworldsmen', and he regarded them as a threat to his new positive morality.

The essential thing to appreciate is that Nietzsche wants to set aside all traditional morality and start again. He wants to go beyond the traditional way of assessing behaviour, and to get *Beyond Good and Evil*, the title of a work he published in 1886. The phrase used by Nietzsche for this process was '*the revaluation of all values*'.

4 Master morality and slave morality

Key quote

Two of his aphorisms at the opening of *Twilight of the Idols* (1888) express Nietzsche's determination to find direction in an otherwise directionless world:

'*Even the bravest of us rarely has the courage for what he really knows…*'

'*Formula of my happiness: a Yes, a No, a straight line, a goal…*'

In his book *On the Genealogy of Morals* (1887), Nietzsche sums up themes that he developed earlier. It comprises three 'essays':

- The first deals with the nature of 'good' and 'evil', and in particular with the distinction between slave morality and master morality. In a wonderful image he suggests that, from the perspective of lambs, birds of prey represent all that is 'evil', while their own powerlessness and inability to retaliate becomes 'goodness'.
- The second deals with the origins of guilt and conscience, which he sees as a form of sickness, inhibiting the animal instincts. Such elements of moral consciousness are set in the context of the relationship between the powerful and the powerless. We obey the laws imposed on us because we are powerless to do otherwise, but claim such obedience as goodness.
- The third is an attack on the ascetic ideal, the flight from human potential. He sees the weak, sick 'will', unable to cope with animal instincts, as recognising and making a virtue out of its own insignificance. He famously ends with the claim that man would sooner will nothingness than not will at all. In other words, fleeing from humankind's true potential, people deliberately accept and embrace their own insignificance.

Nietzsche considered that the sort of moral qualities that had been promoted by Christianity – meekness, gentleness, compassion – were features of the morality of slaves, those who were concerned to help one another in a situation of helplessness and suffering. He contrasted such 'slave morality' with 'master morality' which he saw prefigured in the Greek ideal of the good life, which included the sense of nobility and self-development. 'Master morality' sought to develop qualities that would advance humankind; slave morality sought to develop qualities that would protect the weakest in society.

He considered that these two forms of morality gave rise to two different personal attitudes towards the world. Those who followed

Key thought

Nietzsche did not limit his moral criticism to Christianity. He considered that the concepts of justice, equality and compassion, as they had emerged from the Enlightenment, and as they had been presented unchallenged as moral ideals and goals by secular philosophers, were equally the product of slave morality.

master morality would seek to develop themselves, to explore every potential to its limit, and even to give their own lives for the sake of something higher. By contrast, those following slave morality would be mainly concerned with self-preservation.

5 The threat of the Christian ascetic

Nietzsche saw traditional Christian morality as a threat. It appeared to him to inhibit the natural development of strength and, by emphasising the weakness of man, it undermined a fundamentally positive approach to life which would be necessary for strength and nobility to be recognised and approved. Two quotations from his *On the Genealogy of Morals* bring this out:

> *To demand of strength that it should* not *express itself as strength, that it should* not *be a will to overcome, overthrow, dominate, a thirst for enemies and resistance and triumph, makes as little sense as to demand of weakness that it should express itself as strength.*
>
> (First essay, section 13)

> *The* sickly *constitute the greatest danger to man:* not *the evil,* not *the 'predators'. Those who are from the outset victims, downtrodden, broken – they are the ones, the* weakest *are the ones who most undermine life among men, who most dangerously poison and question our trust in life, in man.*
>
> (Third essay, section 14)

The problem is that those who suffer think that they are to blame for their suffering. The concept of being a sinner haunts Nietzsche, for it creates a sense of guilt as a response to suffering, and this is encouraged by what he calls the **ascetic** ideal. 'Someone must be to blame for the fact that I do not feel well' is how he describes the thinking of those who are sickly, and – encouraged by religion – they blame themselves as sinners for their plight. But the fact that someone feels guilty does not prove that he or she *should* be guilty. Guilt is interpretation, not fact, but it is an interpretation that Nietzsche ascribes to Christian morality.

Ascetic ideals are hostile to life. Nietzsche sees them within the Judaeo-Christian tradition and the secular forms of them accepted in the Western philosophy he saw around him. It is these anti-life ideals that he considers to be poisoning the life of the state.

Although he saw its influence as harmful, Nietzsche also recognised the power of the ascetic ideal (which is based on the slave morality) and asks why it should have gained such influence. His answer is that it provides something to fill the void of a world without meaning, and to give some consolation in the face of meaningless suffering:

Key word

Ascetic: one who deliberately seeks hardship or practises severe self-discipline, for a personal or spiritual purpose.

This young monk in Thailand has chosen to live a life of disciplined simplicity for a fixed period of time. Do you see his choice as positive or negative?

For the meaning of the ascetic ideal is none other than this: *that something was missing, that man was surrounded by a gaping* void – *he did not know how to justify, explain, affirm himself, he suffered from the problem of his meaning.*

The meaninglessness of suffering, and not suffering as such, has been the curse that has hung over mankind up to now – *and the ascetic ideal offered mankind a meaning!*

and he ends with:

… man would rather will nothingness *than not will at all…*
(Third essay, section 28)

In other words – and we shall return to this in the next chapter, on existentialism – humankind revolts from the idea of complete meaninglessness. It would rather accept a negative attitude to life than have no attitude at all. It craves meaning, even if the meaning it is offered is laden with a sense of personal guilt and unworthiness.

Nietzsche and Marx

Notice the parallels between Nietzsche's criticism of religion's slave morality and Marx's criticism of the place of religion in society. Marx – in the famous passage in his *Introduction to the Critique of the Hegelian Philosophy of Right* – described religion as:

… the sigh of the oppressed creature, the feelings of a heartless world, just as it is the spirit of unspiritual conditions. It is the opium of the people. The abolition of religion as the illusory happiness of the people is required for their real happiness.

- Marx saw religion as holding people back from improving their actual conditions by promising them a substitute happiness. He judged that, deprived of such substitutes, people would face the reality of their situation and therefore be motivated to develop themselves and gain actual happiness.
- Nietzsche is really saying much the same thing, except that his context is the nature of mankind and its movement towards the Superman. People should not feel held back by religion but should strive to develop themselves.
- But Marx, of course, sees change as arising as a result of class struggle, whereas Nietzsche is concerned with the individual as a member of the whole human species in its movement forward.

Nietzsche's criticism of Church morality is made clear in a section entitled 'Morality as Anti-nature' in *Twilight of the Idols*:

The Church combats the passions with excision in every sense of the word: its practice, its 'cure' is castration. It never asks: 'How can one spiritualise, beautify, deify a desire?' – it has at all times laid the emphasis of its discipline on extirpation (of sensuality, of pride, of lust

Key thought

But recognise how radically
different that sort of morality is
from, for example, utilitarianism.
To find a morality of this sort, we
need to go back to Aristotle's
ideas, in which the concept of
good included those of perfection
and nobility.

*for power, of avarice, of revengefulness). But to attack the passions at
their roots means to attack life at its roots: the practice of the Church
is hostile to life…*

It is debatable whether the Church, now or then, actually took that
view of the passions, but the positive side of this criticism is that
Nietzsche wants to explore a morality that would allow natural
human passions to be channelled creatively and encourage us to be
forever going beyond ourselves.

6 The eternal recurrence

Key thought

'The eternal recurrence' is one of
the more difficult of Nietzsche's
concepts. What he is saying is that
the Superman should be quite
prepared to say 'Yes' to living this
same life over and over again, just
as it is, forever – a radical
acceptance of the reality of the
here and now.

Everything in the world is linked together – happiness and sorrow,
success and tragic failure – and one cannot accept some parts of it
without accepting them all. For Nietzsche, the triumph of the
Superman (and indeed, it would seem, of anyone who can say 'Yes'
wholeheartedly to anything) is this absolute and positive affirmation
of the world just as it is, however much pain it might involve. And
in affirming this, Nietzsche returns to the idea that the Superman
shall become the meaning of the earth. Whatever meaning and
purpose there is in life, it is given that meaning by humankind.
There is no God; no external guarantor or provider of meaning.

The eternal recurrence presents those who think morally with a
fundamental question: Are you attempting, through your ideals and
sense of what is 'good', to escape from the reality of the world as it
is? Or are you prepared to say 'Yes' to the mixture of experiences,
both happy and painful, that are the reality of life, and within that
context exercise your will in order to shape your own destiny?

7 A challenge and a problem

Key thought

Nietzsche's ethical theory presents
a clear challenge both to religious
ideas of morality, and also to
utilitarianism, natural law and any
other attempt to find a fixed and
objective basis for ethics.

The positive morality of the Superman is a morality that accepts life
just as it is, and says 'Yes' to it, that develops itself to the limit, and is
not deflected by self-pity or any substitute, other-worldly goals. The
only criterion for moral action is self-transcendence – to develop
yourself, going beyond what you are now. But here there is a
fundamental problem: What exactly should you develop?

We saw in Chapter 10 that Kant presented the categorical
imperative as a principle that one should only do something if you
could will at the same time that everyone else should be free to
follow the same principle. In other words, one's action became
morally good if done with conviction, and without the prospect of
self-contradiction if universalised. But that only gives the framework
within which morality operates, it does not say exactly *what* should

be done. The same problem occurs with Nietzsche. It is easy to see the sort of slave morality that he regards as weakening humanity. He is not happy with compassion, equality and justice. But what exactly is to go in their place? How is it possible for everyone to seek self-transcendence? What could it mean in practice?

Postscript to Nietzsche

With the rise of Fascism in Germany and Italy, some of Nietzsche's ideas were used to justify nationalist and racist views about the superiority of the Aryan race, views which led to the horrors of the Holocaust. Both Mussolini and Hitler read Nietzsche.

In order that Nietzsche's thought is not simply identified with those later ideologies, it is important to recognise that Nietzsche himself – as far as we know from his writings – was not racist, and his criticism of the Jews was part of his broader criticism of religion. The idea of identifying the development of the Superman with one particular racial group is foreign to Nietzsche's thinking, in which everyone and every group is required to be constantly going beyond itself.

On the other hand, the later misuse of Nietzsche's writings highlights the problem raised above. His ethical thought gives direction but not specific content – except in the negative sense of having criticised justice, equality and compassion as being the product of slave morality. That, along with the very style of his writing, makes him open to a variety of dangerous interpretations.

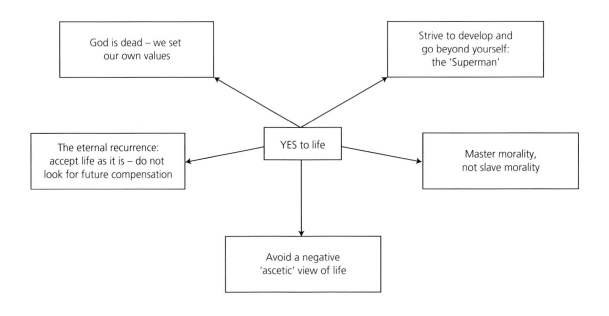

God is dead – we set our own values

Strive to develop and go beyond yourself: the 'Superman'

The eternal recurrence: accept life as it is – do not look for future compensation

YES to life

Master morality, not slave morality

Avoid a negative 'ascetic' view of life

Study guide

By the end of this chapter you should have a general understanding of key features of Nietzsche's view of morality, and be able to consider these in the light of other moral theories outlined in this book. In particular, you are encouraged to reflect on the nature of the self and its development, and the origins of concepts such as 'good', 'evil' and 'conscience'.

Revision checklist ✓

Can you explain...?

- Why, for Nietzsche, the death of God leads to the need for the 'Superman'.
- What Nietzsche meant by 'slave morality' and 'master morality'.
- Why Nietzsche saw weakness as a threat.

Do you know...?

- Why Nietzsche thought it important to reject the idea of compensation in a future life.
- Why Nietzsche saw guilt as harmful.

Give arguments for and against...

- The idea that the moral duty of humankind is to develop itself into something higher.

Examples of essay questions

1. Outline the distinction Nietzsche made between slave and master morality. Why did he see Christian moral teaching as 'slave' morality? Do you consider his criticisms of Christianity justified?

AO1 would require a clear understanding of the two forms of morality, and why Nietzsche saw Christianity as promoting 'slave' morality. Higher levels would draw out the distinction between the two moralities.

AO2 should be focused on Nietzsche's argument, exploring its weaknesses and strengths. It would not be sufficient simply to state an independent argument in favour of Christianity.

*2. 'The Superman shall be the meaning of the earth.'
How does Nietzsche's view of the goal of human life in
terms of the 'Superman' relate to his ethics? Do you
consider his argument persuasive?*

AO1 really requires some background in the 'death of God' and the
perception of humankind as part of an evolutionary process, and a
clear presentation of the goal of the 'Superman'. The establishment
of that goal can then be shown to justify 'master morality'.

AO2 will require an evaluation of the idea of setting the future
of humankind as the ultimate goal, and also whether such a goal
provides a valid basis for ethics. Higher level candidates might
compare it with other theories, such as natural law or utilitarianism.

Further questions

1 Explain how Nietzsche's ethical theory presents a challenge to
utilitarianism. How successful is this challenge?

2 Explain Nietzsche's concept of 'eternal recurrence'. To what extent
are other moral theories, with their focus on ideals and 'the good',
just attempts to escape from the reality of the world as it is?

Chapter checklist ✓

In this chapter we shall review the ethical theories covered so far and then move on to consider the ethical implications of existentialism, as exemplified in the writings of Kierkegaard, Heidegger and Sartre.

1 Introduction

If we review for a moment the bases upon which philosophers have sought to establish their theories of right and wrong, we find that they are:

1 The sense of justice within society
2 The quest for happiness
3 The structure and purpose of the natural order
4 The emotions, and natural sense of altruism
5 Contractual agreements between people
6 The expected results of action
7 The pure practical reason
8 The will.

Key word

Altruism: a natural, unselfish disposition to do good to others.

The first, third, fifth and sixth of these are independent of an individual's moral sensitivities; they attempt to give an overall way of assessing moral goodness which people might agree on through rational argument. The second was based on Aristotle's view of what constituted the good life, and the sense of the potential, both personal and social that a person should strive to realise. The fourth takes as its starting point people's natural sense of right and wrong, and their **altruism** – in particular the feeling that people in need ought to be helped, even at the cost of one's own immediate happiness.

But in all these there is the problem of trying to establish an 'ought' from an 'is'. We saw how both Hume and G. E. Moore used this as a major criticism of existing moral systems. The good cannot be defined in terms of either structure, emotions, agreement or results, because it would then be possible to go on and ask if and why that structure, emotion, agreement or result was itself 'good', and so on ad infinitum. In other words, there needed to be some intuition of 'good', simple and indefinable, to underpin all such systems.

The remaining possibilities we looked at for establishing a basis of ethics were therefore the pure practical reason (Kant) or the will (Nietzsche). Following this line of thinking, we take responsibility for our actions and for shaping our future. We do not try to discover what is right and good and then apply it to ourselves, allowing it to determine what we want to do. Rather, it is our reason or our will which determines what is good.

In all these theories there is a balance between the needs and desires of the individual and those of the society within which he or she lives. Some emphasise the role of society: ethics being established by mutual agreement, or by the assessment of those results that offer the greatest benefit to the maximum number of people. Others (e.g. Kant or Nietzsche) start with the individual, and then show how individual morality relates to society – in Kant's case by thinking of everyone as 'ends' rather than 'means'; in Nietzsche's case, by seeing 'going beyond' yourself as part of an overall forward movement of humankind. How then do we give our lives meaning and purpose? And how does that relate to an overall meaning and purpose of society? Or, indeed, is life meaningless and with it all sense of morality?

It is this line of questioning that brings us on to **existentialism**, an approach to these questions which is generally thought of as starting a little before the time of Nietzsche, with the work of a Danish philosopher and theologian, Kierkegaard.

Key thought

Of course, there can be guidelines for directing that will – for Kant, the categorical imperative; for Nietzsche, the responsibility to go beyond oneself.

Key question

Should we start our ethical thinking with the individual or with society, and what is the right balance between them?

Key word

Existentialism: philosophy concerned with the nature and meaning of human existence.

2 Søren Kierkegaard

Key people

Georg Hegel (1770–1831) was an influential German philosopher, who saw history as the unfolding of a dynamic process of change, leading to an ultimate goal, and open to rational examination.

Key word

Dialectic: the process of thesis, antithesis and synthesis that Hegel saw as the basic structure of change.

The philosopher Hegel, who was very influential at the time of Kierkegaard, saw everything in terms of a broad collective process and movement. He is best known for his **dialectic**, in which a 'thesis' leads on to its opposite, an 'antithesis', resolving finally in a 'synthesis.' Every aspect of human life was set within this overall process. Thus an individual becomes an example of a particular phase in social change, only to be understood by setting him or her within a social context and movement.

Kierkegaard rejected this. He was a very religious man, and insisted that the key relationship was of an individual with God, and that God had given people freedom to make their own decisions. He therefore wanted to show that our existence is not something determined rationally, nor simply part of an ongoing process or abstract system,

Key people

Søren Kierkegaard (1813–55)

A deeply troubled and sensitive thinker, Kiekegaard rejected the then fashionable philosophy of Hegel, arguing that it was too impersonal, and did not do justice to the responsibility and inward experience of the individual in making decisions about matters of belief and behaviour. In response, he published *Either/Or* (1843), soon followed by *Fear and Trembling* and *Philosophical Fragments*. His emphasis on the very personal nature of the relationship between individuals, the things they believe and the choices they make, opened up a new dimension in philosophy: existentialism.

Key thoughts

Central to existentialism is the idea that we have an active part to play in shaping ourselves, and that life is a constant process of becoming, in which our decisions are the agents of change.

Kierkegaard emphasised the responsibility and challenge of individual choice in shaping people's lives.

but is something quite specific. His philosophy starts with the individual and the values and choices that he or she makes. He saw human existence as something that was created and shaped by personal choices:

> *If you will understand me aright, I should like to say that in making a choice it is not so much a question of choosing the right as of the energy, the earnestness, the pathos with which one chooses. Thereby the personality announces its inner infinity, and thereby, in turn, the personality is consolidated. Therefore, even if a man were to choose the wrong, he will nevertheless discover, precisely by reason of the energy with which he chose, that he had chosen the wrong. For the choice being made with the whole inwardness of his personality, his nature is purified and he himself brought into immediate relation to the external Power whose omnipresence interpenetrates the whole of existence.*
>
> *(Either/Or, 1843)*

Kierkegaard is therefore generally regarded as the founder of existentialism. This is a school of philosophy which is concerned with the nature of human existence and with its meaning.

Kierkegaard recognised, however, that taking such responsibility was not easy. He saw our freedom as something quite terrifying. It was an act of faith, a leap in the dark, to make a choice; and yet one could not escape from it. He regarded those (e.g. Hegel) who formed abstract schemes of thought by which to comprehend life and give to every action some place in an overall pattern, as in some way escapist. The real challenge of life was not to be found in speculation, nor in a structure that could guarantee that a decision was right, but in the actual process of acting and making choices. In other words, his challenge to ethical thinking is that one cannot understand moral choice by standing back and assessing it, but only by engaging in choices, conscious of the freedom to make a difference and to shape ourselves.

3 Martin Heidegger

Key thought

Kierkegaard regarded becoming an individual as a challenge, and a person's 'good' as whatever enabled him or her to become a true individual.

Kierkegaard was a religious man, but one who felt that God had given to the individual the terrifying prospect of individual responsibility and choice. By contrast, Heidegger (like Nietzsche before him) approached the situation of human awareness and choice from an atheistic point of view, although he had a religious upbringing and originally studied theology. But there is another important difference: Kierkegaard presents the sort of ethical choices we make as though each of them is absolute and free; Heidegger recognised that most of our choices relate to existing relationships and commitments that are already established and presented to us.

Key people

Martin Heidegger (1889–1976)
was controversial because of his
support for the Nazi party in the
1930s. He contributed key features
to existential philosophy. He was
concerned with the question of
what it means to be, as an
individual with a particular set of
circumstances, a set of hopes for
the future, and the temptation to
fall into the various roles that
society provides. His most important
work is *Being and Time*, 1927.

Key word

Geworfenheit: Heidegger's term
for the 'thrown-ness' of existence:
the fact that we are born into a
particular set of circumstances.

Key question

What is the real me, beneath
these masks and social roles? How
can I live an authentic existence?

Thus, for Heidegger, we start from that given set of circumstances in
which we find ourselves. These are not part of some divine plan, but
are just given as an accident of birth. His term for this is 'thrown-
ness' (*Geworfenheit*). From the moment of our birth we are thrown
into a set of conditions within which to live – we have not chosen
them, they are just there. We are part of the world, and our choices
are made as part of that world.

As we face other people, we form an image of them in our
mind. That image is not the actual person (we cannot know them
fully) but is like a mask we impose on them. One might think in
terms of those who perform a function – being a milkman, a
solicitor, an accountant, a shop assistant. The person I meet is far
more than that social function, but nevertheless, that is all I know at
present, and therefore I react to them on that basis. Equally, of
course, a person may have the mask of 'wife', 'husband', 'son',
'daughter', 'lover', 'stranger' or 'enemy'. And, of course, as they look
at us, other people project onto us the same sort of masks. When I
come to make choices, when I act, how should I behave? Should I
conform to what other people expect of me? Should I play at being
what they expect? If so, do I lose my integrity?

Choices! Choices! We are thrown into life and stride forward, but with a bewildering number of options –
staircases leading to different destinations. Freedom to choose can be threatening and confusing, but we
have no option but to choose, to be carried forward and to live with the results.

Key thought

We are thrown into our particular
life by the circumstances of our
birth, and the only certainty about
our future is that we will die. The
challenge is to know how to
achieve an authentic existence in
the brief space in between!

These are the key questions for an existential approach to life and in
particular to ethics. Existentialism combines a sense of the importance
of exercising the will (as Nietzsche) and of recognising the freedom
that choice implies (as Kierkegaard) but it also recognises that we do
not exercise our wills, nor are we free, in a vacuum. We are thrown
into our particular circumstances. We are given a set of roles to
perform, and we realise that our lives are seen in a limited way by

others. In the light of all this, I need to escape the expectation of others and affirm my own authentic existence and freedom.

There is an additional motivation to start taking responsibility for our lives, that is the fact of death. Heidegger makes the point that it is anxiety in the face of the inevitability of death, and therefore the very limited nature of our life, that motivates us.

4 Jean-Paul Sartre

Key people

Jean-Paul Sartre (1905–80)
was a cultural phenomenon and a dominant thinker in Paris in the years following the Second World War. As well as philosophy, he wrote novels, plays, literary criticism and was actively involved in political issues. His major philosophical works are *Being and Nothingness*, 1943, and *Critique of Dialectical Reason*, 1960.

Key thought

Existence precedes essence.

Key quote

'Hell is other people.'
                                SARTRE, *NO EXIT*

Key thought

In his 'natural law' approach to ethics Aquinas considered essence to precede existence. Thus everything has a purpose, and that purpose is an inherent part of its design or function. An action is morally right if it fulfils its allotted purpose. Aquinas believed in a purposeful creator God, and therefore assumed that everything is created with a purpose that it should fulfil. But Sartre takes an atheistic position. There is no generalised sense of purpose or design that can automatically be applied to objects, events or people.

Like Heidegger, Sartre emphasised the creative role of an individual in shaping himself or herself. He did this by emphasising that, for human beings, existence comes before and shapes their essence, not the other way round. On the other hand, if you consider any inanimate object that is the product of human design, it is clear that the essence of that object (be it a car or a television, for example) was determined before it came into existence. After all, people do not simply create objects and then wonder what to do with them; a car is created as a car – that is its essence, and that determines what will be done with it once it comes into existence. For all such objects, their essence precedes their existence.

Sartre took the view that human beings, in what they do and the choices they make, shape their own lives. There is no fixed 'essence' of me that I must discover and live up to. Rather, 'I' am something that will develop a particular character, an essence, as I go through life. My essence grows through my existence. In his famous phrase, which sums up what existentialism is about: *existence precedes essence*.

But Sartre held that we choose our emotions and our motivations, and that these may be traced back to an 'original choice' that is the basis of motivation and which must therefore itself be unmotivated. But such a choice would be 'absurd'. Therefore, however reasonable and directed subsequent choices and motives would seem to be, all our life is fundamentally based on the absurd. It cannot be rationally justified in terms of anything else.

Like Heidegger, it is important for Sartre that a person should not simply accept the roles that others might allocate, but should allow his or her sense of self to expand outwards to take in the things that are experienced. We are free to choose how we act, and that freedom is absolutely key to Sartre's view of the individual; to reject that freedom and its responsibility is to act in 'bad faith'.

Sartre sees human consciousness as '*être-pour-soi*' (being for itself), which is contrasted with the things of which we are conscious, which are '*être-en-soi*' (being in itself). This distinction is very important, for it characterises two different ways of being in the world. It is possible to become aware of the external world, to reflect upon it and relate to it in such a way that it becomes part of

Key thought

In the act of choosing, according to Sartre, you make clear the values that you hold for humankind in general.

one's own consciousness: *être-pour-soi*. On the other hand, it is possible to refuse to take any active engagement with experience, and simply accept the roles that other people impose on you. In this case, you become an object: *être-en-soi*.

> *In fact, in creating the man that we want to be, there is not a single one of our acts which does not at the same time create an image of man as we think he ought to be. To choose to be this or that is to affirm at the same time the value of what we choose, because we can never choose evil. We always choose the good, and nothing can be good for us without being good for all.*
>
> (*Existentialism and Human Emotions*, 1957)

The existential task is to develop and take in new experiences, shaping oneself all the time. Life is a challenge and a project. In practice, however, Sartre took the view that one should allow to everyone else the freedom that one wished for oneself, thus creating a basis of mutual respect between oneself and other people.

5 Simone de Beauvoir

Key people

Simone de Beauvoir (1908–86) Like Sartre, with whom she had a relationship that started when they met as students, Simone de Beauvoir was both a philosopher and a novelist. Her book *The Second Sex*, 1949, was hugely influential in the modern feminist movement.

Key word

Intentionality: this is the view that consciousness is not just a sequence of sense impressions, but is always 'about' something; as we encounter the world we seek to make sense of it and see how it relates to us.

Key thought

If our consciousness is always ambiguous, the quest for certainty is futile and doomed to failure.

In *The Ethics of Ambiguity*, 1947, Simone de Beauvoir presents our relationship with the world in terms of **intentionality**. This is the idea, commonly used in the philosophy of mind, to express the way in which, as we become conscious of the world, we seek to understand and make sense of it, and – at the same time – we engage with the world and want to give it a meaning of our own choosing. In other words, our consciousness of the world is not just a succession of phenomena to be experienced in some detached way, but is all about the intention we have to find and give meaning to what we experience.

But the key thing about this intentionality is that it is always *ambiguous*; we never fully succeed either in finding meaning in the world or in giving it meaning. This has clear implications for ethics, because other ethical theories have tried to define and give certainty to matters of right and wrong.

Hence, for de Beauvoir, all ethics should acknowledge that the future is uncertain and open; our ethics must acknowledge that our experience of moral choice is a matter of hope, rather than certainty. The key theme here is freedom. As a child, I am born into a world of ready-made rules and regulations, but as I grow to adulthood, I am challenged to accept that I am free and responsible. To deny that freedom, or to retreat into the childish patters of simply accepting given rules, is to act in bad faith. But ethics involves other people, and an awareness of my own freedom requires that I accept the freedom of others too, and engage with them in projects to achieve common goals.

6 Ethical implications of the existentialist approach

Key quote

'The existentialist ... thinks it very distressing that God does not exist, because all possibility of finding values in a heaven of ideas disappears along with Him; there can no longer be an a priori Good, *since there is no infinite and perfect consciousness to think it. Nowhere is it written that the* Good *exists, that we must be honest, that we must not lie; because the fact is we are on a plane where there are only men. Dostoevsky said, "If God didn't exist, everything would be possible." That is the very starting point of existentialism. Indeed, everything is permissible if God does not exist, and as a result man is forlorn, because neither within him nor without does he find anything to cling to. He can't start making excuses for himself.'*
SARTRE, *EXISTENTIALISM AND HUMAN EMOTIONS*, 1957

So far we have looked at the sort of views about human life and its choices that characterise existentialism. Clearly these have implications for ethics. First of all, it is clear that individuals have their own projects, and the choices they make reflect these. Existentialism therefore rejects the imposition of moral codes: rather each person has to decide for himself or herself. It is most important to reject all attempts to have masks or images imposed on us; we should be free to reject all conventions.

It is clear that a person has to accept responsibility for his or her decisions, and the implication of such freedom is that it should allow the same freedom to others. Thus it would be inconsistent to reject conventions that other people might want to impose on me, but at the same time seek to impose them on others.

On the other hand, this rejection of all external aids and structures, although it emphasises freedom, is not an easy option. It brings both responsibility and a sense of loneliness, for we have to find within ourselves the courage to make choices and live with the results. We are what we make of ourselves – and that can be quite daunting.

If I think of myself as part of that external world (what Kant called the world of phenomena), then I make myself an object, part of other people's *être-en-soi*, to use Sartre's term. Once that happens, I lose my freedom; I become part of a determined system of cause and effect. My awareness of myself as a free and responsible agent disappears.

What existentialism keeps open is the awareness of the significance of what happens when a person makes a choice. It is a point of freedom and of responsibility, it is an expression of that person's individual existence, and at the same time it is the point at which his or her values are expressed.

Key thought

I act within the world, I do not simply watch while the world offers me ready planned options, or allow it to determine what I should do.

a) The context

It might be worth reflecting on the fact that the period during which existentialism developed as a philosophy corresponded to the time when conventional ethical statements were being challenged from a linguistic point of view. The logical positivist attack on moral statements, leading to emotive and prescriptive interpretations of what moral statements were actually about, helped to move the climate of thought away from morality as existing 'out there' in some way, to seeing it as a human project, as an expression of human wishes, emotions or recommendations for action (see p.38).

Existentialism may be seen as the conclusion of a line of argument that goes back to Kant – that, over against the world of

Key thought

Meta-ethics matched up quite conveniently with existentialism in the mid-twentieth century. This fact, however, was not always recognised, since existentialism was very much a phenomenon of 'Continental' philosophy, while meta-ethics thrived mainly within the Anglo-American analytic tradition.

my experience, there is an immediate awareness of my freedom to make choices. Those choices, and the freedom to make them, come from within myself as an experiencing and willing agent, they are not simply derived from the external world of experience.

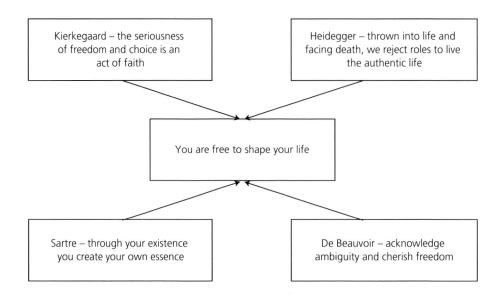

Kierkegaard – the seriousness of freedom and choice is an act of faith

Heidegger – thrown into life and facing death, we reject roles to live the authentic life

You are free to shape your life

Sartre – through your existence you create your own essence

De Beauvoir – acknowledge ambiguity and cherish freedom

Study guide

By the end of this chapter you should have a general view of the way in which existentialist philosophers see the creative importance of freedom and choice, and therefore why they avoid any fixed or legalistic approach to moral questions.

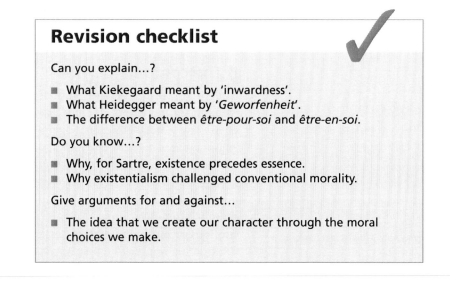

Revision checklist

Can you explain...?

- What Kiekegaard meant by 'inwardness'.
- What Heidegger meant by '*Geworfenheit*'.
- The difference between *être-pour-soi* and *être-en-soi*.

Do you know...?

- Why, for Sartre, existence precedes essence.
- Why existentialism challenged conventional morality.

Give arguments for and against...

- The idea that we create our character through the moral choices we make.

Examples of essay questions

1. The freedom of existentialism to create one's own values is an easy option. Discuss.

AO1 might include reference to Kierkegaard, who certainly regarded existential choice as a serious matter, or Heidegger's emphasis on authenticity rather than accepting roles.

AO2 requires a balanced assessment of whether the challenge of creating one's own values is harder than accepting and obeying existing moral principles.

2. According to Heidegger, we are thrown into life with a particular set of circumstances within which to make our choices. We are also expected to conform to the expectations other people have of us. Does this imply that we are never completely free to be ourselves? How might this relate to the moral choices a person makes?

For AO1, although it is useful to start with Heidegger, this question leads on to the more general question about self-identity. Higher level answers might bring in issues of freedom and determinism (as discussed in Chapter 3), or Kant's idea that we are phenomenally determined but noumenally free.

AO2 requires some conclusion about whether or not we are ever absolutely free, and whether the choices we make when we have less than total freedom are morally significant.

Further questions

1 Examine the strengths and weaknesses of the existentialist approach to morality.

2 To what extent is it possible to resist conforming to social roles?

13 SITUATION ETHICS

Chapter checklist

In this chapter we shall look at 'situation ethics' and the meaning of 'agape' and assess the strengths and weaknesses of this theory.

1 Introduction

Key thought

This method of argument is sometimes called **casuistry**, as we saw above in connection with Aquinas (p.66).

Key word

Casuistry: the application of general principles to specific examples.

Key quote

'That which is done out of love always takes place beyond good and evil.'

NIETZSCHE, *BEYOND GOOD AND EVIL*, 153

In the 1960s, both in the USA and in Europe, there was a widespread reaction against what was seen as the narrowness of traditional morality. It was a time of social change and of a quest for freedom and self-expression. One book which reflected that social change was Joseph Fletcher's *Situation Ethics* (1966). In it he opposed a deductive method of ethical reasoning: that is, he felt that it was unwise to start from fixed rules and then deduce from them what should be done in any particular situation.

On the other hand, Fletcher wanted to maintain what he saw as the fundamental feature of Christian morality, the law of love. He therefore argued that there should be a single and simple principle, in the light of which individuals could work out what was right for their particular circumstances, and the situations in which they found themselves. *He claimed that the only absolute rule was that of love. In any given situation, the right thing to do was that which love required.*

Of course, he recognised that people would not always be able to decide what was right without help, and he conceded that rules could help to inform a person's decision. Nevertheless, ultimately, it was not the rules that counted but the principle of love. Thus, where love demanded that a conventional moral rule should be set aside, it was right to do so. Rules could not be absolutely or universally valid.

Fletcher sets out four working principles for situation ethics:

- *Pragmatism:* The 'pragmatists' were philosophers who argued that the truth of a statement should be judged by whether it 'worked', in other words whether positive results came if it were

Key people

Joseph Fletcher (1905–91)
was an academic and an ordained priest in the American Episcopal Church. He taught Christian Ethics, and took a liberal attitude towards moral issues, including euthanasia, abortion and contraception. His controversial book *Situation Ethics* was published in 1966 and provoked criticism from those of a more conservative Christian moral standpoint. He became Professor of Medical Ethics at the University of Virginia and took a particular interest in the ethical aspect of genetics.

Key thought

Relativism: clearly, situation ethics will always have elements of relativism, since it rejects the imposition of moral rules on individual situations, but it is not completely relativist, since it accepts the primacy of the law of love. Fletcher described his system as one of 'situational or contextual decision-making'.

Key thought

To some extent, Fletcher can be seen as following an early tradition within Christian moral thought.

Key quote

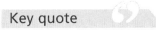

'Love and do what you like.'
ST AUGUSTINE

taken to be true. Fletcher's first working principle is similar, in that he argues that a moral theory needs to be judged according to whether it can produce good practical results.

- *Relativism*: He does not want a fully relativist system (which would be to reject all moral rules or principles) but argued that the basic law of love should be applied in a way that is relative to each individual situation.
- *Positivism*: Fletcher accepted that moral choices themselves cannot be verified (this had been argued by the logical positivists), but said that they could be *vindicated*. In other words, they can be shown to work and to put into effect the basic commitment to the law of love.
- *Personalism*: Whereas a strictly legalist approach can be impersonal in its application of absolute rules, Fletcher wants to look at each situation and ask who needs to be helped.

His theory is also conveniently summarised in six propositions that logically follow on from one another. These are:

- Love is the only intrinsic value.
- The norm for Christian moral decision-making is to put love first.
- Love is the same as justice – because justice is 'love distributed'.
- Love wills the good of the other person, whether we like or approve of them or not.
- The end justifies the means (here Fletcher moves towards utilitarianism and becomes vulnerable to the criticisms of that theory, namely that results are often ambiguous and provisional).
- It is the situation which determines what love requires, it cannot be prescribed in advance.

In the earliest days of the Christian Church, the break with Judaism involved setting aside strict moral and social codes. The early Christians claimed that their fellowship was based on love, and that it was therefore able to transcend barriers that separated people of very different social and religious backgrounds. An expression of love taking priority is seen, for example, in the famous thirteenth chapter *I Corinthians*. There is also the well-known saying of St Augustine that if you love you can do what you like, which did not imply freedom, so much as the trust that whatever was fully motivated by love would be morally right.

A similar approach was taken by others. The theologian Paul Tillich, for example, wrote a short book in 1963 entitled *Morality and Beyond* in which he argued that if there were no rules, people would always have to work out time and again what was the right thing for them to do, and that in practical terms this would be

Key people

Paul Tillich (1886–1965)
taught in universities in Germany and then the United States. He was influenced by existentialists such as Kierkegaard and Heidegger. He took a radical look at Christian teachings, and expressed them in modern philosophical terms.

impossible. Therefore (like Fletcher) he accepted that there could be rules, but that they should offer guidance only.

For Tillich, religion was about a person's 'ultimate concern' – that which he or she held to be of ultimate value in life – and his moral argument here links moral choice to that ultimate concern. In the end, there is something higher than the morality of obeying rules, and whether it is one's 'ultimate concern' or simply an absolute principle of love, it is the striving after some transcendent value that makes an action morally right.

In practice, Tillich's position is rather more conservative than Fletcher's, and is widely adopted (although seldom related directly to Tillich himself). It represents a balance between Fletcher and conventional rule-based systems, and is a recognition that rules are useful, but only when informed by – and where necessary open to the possibility of being changed in the light of – ultimate values.

2 The meaning of 'love'

Key word

Agapeism: (from the Greek *agape*) morality based on love.

Key quote

'Christianity gave Eros poison to drink – he did not die of it, to be sure, but degenerated into vice.
NIETZSCHE, *BEYOND GOOD AND EVIL*, 168

The term 'love' is notoriously ambiguous in English, embracing everything from the Greek term *eros* (erotic love) to *philia* (friendship). Here, the sort of love spoken about is best summed up in the Greek term *agape* (selfless love), and a moral theory that applies love to each situation can therefore be called **agapeism**.

It is also important to recognise that love (in the sense in which it is used in moral arguments) is not simply a matter of the emotions. It is not the same as being 'in love', which may perhaps be regarded as a form of madness in which a particular object of desire utterly dominates a person's emotional life. Love, in the sense that it is used here, involves the rational as well as the emotional. It is the recognition of the value of the loved object in and for itself. It is – to take an expression from *I Corinthians* – not selfish. In other words, it is not a self-indulgent emotion that happens to have latched onto an external object, but a recognition of that object as separate from oneself but held to be of value.

3 Evaluating situation ethics

a) Its advantages

- It is easy to understand: you follow a single principle.
- It gives a person freedom to differ from the decisions of others without feeling that they have thereby done anything wrong, or that they need to give a full justification for that decision. In other words, it is flexible.

- It enables an emotional and rational response to determine what is right in any given situation. In other words, you don't have to follow a conventional moral rule, if that goes against your deepest sense of what love requires.
- It is based on love which, rationally as well as emotionally, is a key feature of all moral systems.

b) Its disadvantages

- The law of love is still a law. Not everyone may be bothered, or have the strength of character, to ask what love requires in a situation. Situation ethics replaces a multitude of rules by a single one – but one that is as easily broken as any other.
- It is difficult to know how two people, who differ about what they see as the demands of love in a particular situation, can engage in meaningful discussion. There is no objective basis upon which one can say that *this* intuition about love is more relevant or valid than *that* one. In other words, there is a danger that it can lead to moral vagueness, with everyone (at the time when this view gained popularity) happy about peace, love, flared trousers, flowers and long hair, but nobody able to specify how such love should be made effective in difficult or ambiguous situations where a shared commitment to a moral position is required.
- It tends to fragment complex moral situations into the individual moral choices where love is applied. At some point, it may be necessary to stand back and take a cool look at all the repercussions of a moral choice. Reason may suggest that something is done which goes against one's immediate feelings, but which, in the wider scheme of things, is seen as right.
- It suffers from the same limitations of other consequentialist theories – namely that we may guess, but are never certain of the results that will follow from a moral choice. Hence, Fletcher's 'pragmatic' principle has its limitations.

c) Rules verses situations

Although we have examined situation ethics in terms of Joseph Fletcher and Paul Tillich's work, we should note that the debate about the place of rules as opposed to the particular situation has a long history.

Thus, for example, the positive aspect of casuistry, in applying general moral rules to particular situations, recognised that rules needed interpretations, and that no two situations were exactly the same. *The 'problem' with casuistry was not that it was attempted, but that it was imposed.* It was seen as the means by which external (and particularly Church) authority could be imposed on individuals, often with very serious consequences.

Key word

Proportionalism: Tillich argued for a proportionalist approach. It was not that rules should be set aside at whim, but only when the circumstances were sufficient to warrant it. In other words, the balance between accepting general rules and following the unique demands of love in each situation was a matter of proportion, never itself an absolute rule.

Key thought

In Thomas Hardy's novel, *Jude the Obscure*, Jude is prevented from working as a stonemason in a church when it is discovered that he is not married to the person with whom he is living. A moral objection to cohabitation is thus imposed on him, with no attempt to discover his personal circumstances.

Equally, the rejection of Hegel's system by Kierkegaard was an attempt to reinstate the centrality of the individual and the creative nature of his or her choices. And Sartre's insistence that in everything we do we create an image of what we think humankind should be, is another way of relating overall principles to individual choices.

Whereas natural law started with the general principles and then worked its way down to the moral implications of particular actions, so the existentialist insisted that it was from those individual choices that a scheme of values was built up. Situation ethics sits between these two positions, accepting a fundamental moral principle, but also respecting the creative seriousness of the individual moral choice. In this, Fletcher wanted to get a balance between a legalistic system of moral rules and an 'antinomianism' which accepts absolutely no rules or principles.

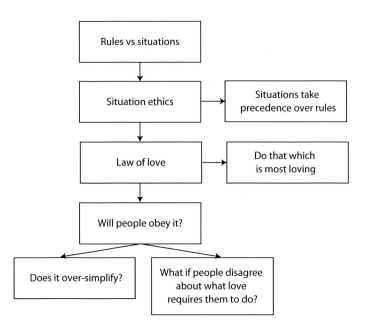

Study guide

By the end of this chapter you should have a clear understanding of the principles upon which Fletcher bases his theory and of the propositions that show how they are put into effect, along with an evaluation of the advantages and disadvantages of this approach. Remember that the context of his work is that of conventional Christian morality facing the requirements of a permissive society.

Revision checklist ✓

Can you explain...?

■ Why Fletcher is critical of casuistry.
■ Why Tillich sees a place for rules.
■ What is meant by 'agapeism'.

Do you know...?

■ Why situation ethics may be accused of simplifying moral dilemmas.
■ Why it may be difficult to argue with someone about a moral issue if both of you use the principles of situation ethics.

Give arguments for and against...

■ Putting situations before moral rules.

Examples of essay questions

1. Do you consider situation ethics, as presented by Fletcher, to be a valid interpretation of traditional Christian ethics? Give your reasons.

AO1 requires a knowledge of the traditional, Christian rule-based approach to moral issues, but also earlier Christian views on the role of love, for example in St Paul, and also St Augustine, as well as a knowledge of the four principles used by Fletcher.

AO2 needs an evaluative assessment of whether Fletcher is following the lead taken by, for example, St Paul.

2. If two people disagree on what is the most loving thing to do, are they both morally right, even if they do very different things in the same situation? Illustrate your answer with reference to at least two practical situations in which there is a moral choice to be made.

AO1 requires two examples both of which have different possible moral choices consistent with 'the most loving thing'. Higher level answers might comment on the difference between general principles – open to wide interpretation – and specific rules, which are easier to apply.

For AO2, since the 'most loving thing' is a very broad principle, you need to argue whether or not you think that any interpretation of it is sufficient to justify a moral choice.

Further questions

1 To what extent can there be absolute moral rules in a multi-ethnic, multicultural and multi-faith society?

2 Can love ever be totally unselfish?

Chapter checklist

In this chapter we shall examine the relationship between religion and ethical theories, the 'Divine Command' theory of ethics, and also look briefly at key features of the ethical approach of the major world religions.

1 Introduction

Ideas about right and wrong, and particularly statements about the nature of the good life, are based (consciously or unconsciously) on a general understanding of the world and of humankind's place in the overall scheme of things. Therefore, it is impossible to ask 'Why should I be moral?' or 'What is the meaning of goodness?' without touching on issues that are also central to religion.

What is more, ethical theories are produced from within a particular culture and historical period, and are therefore influenced by the prevailing modes of thought, including those of religion. It is therefore possible that religion will influence ethics, even where the ethical theory is justified rationally and therefore appears to be quite independent of any religious authority.

If we look back at some of the key thinkers whose work has been outlined in this book, we shall notice that many of them either wrote from within, or in direct opposition to, religion or the moral principles offered by religion. Thus, for example, Augustine and Aquinas were attempting to give reasoned arguments in support of Christian doctrine. Nietzsche and Kierkegaard were both reacting to strict religious upbringing, although taking very different views of religion. Fletcher's situation ethics was clearly a way of modifying a conventional set of religious moral rules to fit with other more radical religious principles, in the context of an increasingly permissive society.

Key thought

In evaluating ethical theories and looking at moral issues generally, we need to be clear about the extent to which the arguments used are based on, or at least influenced by, religious ideas.

2 The relationship between morality and religion

How then are ethics and religion related? There are three possibilities:

- *Autonomy:* An ethical theory is autonomous if it is independent of religion – in other words, if its principles are justified on the basis of reason or experience, without reference to religious concepts. That does not mean that such an ethical theory is opposed to religion, nor does it mean that it cannot be held by someone who is also religious. It is simply to declare that the theory does not require any prior assent to religious ideas. Utilitarianism is autonomous; you can agree with its principles without any reference to religion.

- *Heteronomy:* An ethical theory is heteronomous if it depends upon religious beliefs, or if it has been devised in such a way that it presupposes ideas and values that are given by religion rather than being presented on the basis of reason or experience. So, for example, the Roman Catholic Church has a body of rules called Canon Law. These attempt to deal with the details of behaviour, and to simplify the process of casuistry, by which the principles of natural law would be applied to individual situations. Rules of this sort are made from within a religious community, and are justified in terms of the authority of that community. From an ethical point of view, therefore, they are heteronomous – they originate in religion (even if, subsequently, attempts are made to justify them rationally).

- *Theonomy:* An ethical theory is theonomous if both it and religion depend upon a common source for their principles and values. Western religions speak of the source of principles and values as 'God' (or *theos*, in Greek), so theonomous morality is judged by religious people to come from a fundamental understanding of God, without depending, for example, on the authority of the Church or other religious group. It could be argued that the idea of natural law is theonomous, since both it and theism are based on the idea of an uncaused cause as the creative source of all.

Key word

Canon Law: the word 'canon' comes from the Greek *kanon*, which means 'rule'. In the 1917 Revised Codex of the Roman Catholic Church, there were 2414 of these canons.

Key thought

As presented by Aristotle, ideas about natural law pre-date Christianity, but as Aquinas uses them, they come to be an expression of his belief in God. The same concepts provide the basis for both ethical theory and religious beliefs.

a) Some arguments for moral autonomy

- Obedience to religious rules out of fear of punishment, or abdicating personal responsibility in favour of external religious rules, detracts from personal freedom and choice. Can you really say that you have made a moral choice, if you act out of fear of punishment? If you are motivated by fear, are you free?

- We live in a multi-faith culture. Different religions (or different branches within the same religion) offer different moral rules and regulations, and these may conflict with one another. If you are to make a personal decision, you need to use your reason to assess and choose between them. Such a choice implies a degree of moral autonomy.

- If God is omnipotent (all-powerful) and omniscient (all-knowing), he knows what I am about to choose to do, and would be able to prevent me from making that choice if he wanted to. If I believe this, then I cannot accept sole responsibility for my actions, since God is always an accomplice to my deeds, by making them possible. Moral responsibility requires freedom, and freedom to make decisions and act on them implies moral autonomy.

b) Some arguments for moral heteronomy

- Society is influenced by religious views. Even those who do not profess to follow a religion cannot help but be influenced to some degree. Therefore one needs to admit that a measure of heteronomy is inevitable.
- As soon as you start to define terms like 'good', or use any language about value and purpose, you are dealing with ideas that have long been shaped by religion. You cannot (unless you are going to start from scratch and devise a new vocabulary) present a theory of ethics that is free from the influence of religion. It is therefore more honest to admit this influence.
- It is one thing to come to a conclusion about what you consider to be right or wrong, quite another to have the courage and conviction to put such morality into effect. Only religion, it may be argued, can provide the inspiration to do so.
- Autonomous ethical theories depend on the general good will and reasonableness of people in order for them to take effect. It is one thing to argue that one should seek the greatest happiness for the greatest number, and to show how reasonable such a view is, but if a person is determined to act out of totally selfish motives, there is nothing one can do to prevent them. Religion deals with the dark side of human nature, the negative emotions and rejection of reason. It may be argued that, without the insights of religion, reason cannot produce a workable morality, for it cannot deal effectively with human selfishness.

c) Some arguments for theonomy

- The human impetuses for morality and religion have a common source in 'mystical' awareness, or at least an awareness of things that cannot be described literally. Iris Murdoch, for example, has argued for a fundamental awareness of 'the good' as a basis for morality, and that such awareness continues even in the absence of religion.

A traditional church wedding. Ceremonies to mark birth, marriage and death influence people's views on life, even if they are not particularly religious. Religion and culture influence one another.

Key people

Arthur Schopenhauer (1788–1860)
argued that the idea of separate objects was a feature of time and space, which our senses impose on experiences (as Kant). Beyond the senses, the world is an undifferentiated unity, in which we all share. This unity explains our compassion towards others and our natural ability to understand and respond to people's suffering.

- Philosophers from Schopenhauer (who saw a fundamental unity of all things beneath the multiplicity of sense experience) to G. E. Moore (who argued that the concept 'good' was known by intuition, and was simple – unable to be further defined), have found their ethical systems resting on that which cannot be described rationally, but has to be approached through some form of intuition or immediate awareness. And this, of course, has parallels with religious experience.

- Without some form of fundamental religious or mystical experience, it is difficult to account for the sense of moral obligation, which is experienced almost universally.

- A believer might argue that, if God is rational and if He is the creator of everything (including human reason), then autonomous reason, applied correctly to the world as we experience it, will eventually discover something of God's will and purpose. What appears superficially to be autonomous reason is therefore (from the believer's perspective) actually theonomous, for 'God' may be thought to be found both within and behind it.

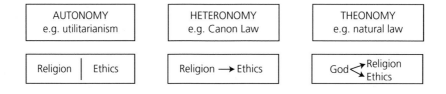

3 Religious authority: the 'Divine Command' theory of ethics

Secular and religious moral systems can often agree on fundamental values, for example 'love' or 'respect for persons'. It is not the moral conclusions that distinguish the secular from the religious, but the methods at which they arrive at those conclusions and the ways in which they justify them.

The 'Divine Command' theory argues that whatever God commands is good. It is linked to the belief that God is the origin of all goodness. Even if that is accepted, however, the problem is to judge exactly how one can know what God commands. If someone argues that personal experience is primary, the conviction that they have had an experience of God commanding something might be totally unverifiable to anyone else, but convincing for them.

On the other hand, if it is argued that a command in the scriptures would count as authoritative, there is the dilemma concerning the way in which the scriptures should be interpreted (literal or otherwise) and the extent to which those scriptures

Key thought

Even if something was
commanded by God 2000 years
ago, does that mean it is
necessarily valid for all time and in
all circumstances?

should be read in the light of circumstances, cultural and historical,
within which they were written. Here the Divine Command theory
is challenged by relativism, which would see religious beliefs and
scriptures as coming from particular settings, and not necessarily
suitable for universal application.

But there is another fundamental problem with the Divine
Command theory, and that is the dilemma about whether God or
'good' should be considered logically primary. It is generally
presented in the form that originates in Plato, known as the
Euthyphro dilemma.

The Euthyphro dilemma

This is so called because it is found in Plato's dialogue *Euthyphro*. In
it, Socrates asks 'Is conduct right because the gods command it, or
do the gods command it because it is right?'

If you argue in favour of the first option, you simply accept that
whatever God commands must be considered 'good': you have no
independent way of deciding right or wrong. Problems occur when
it is believed that God commands something that, in a secular
context, you might want to argue is wrong. For example, there are
cases in the Old Testament when God commands the genocide of
enemies. Is the genocide of enemies therefore to be considered
'good'? You appear to be at the mercy of particular scriptures and
their interpretation.

However, if you do not accept this, and take the second of
Socrates' options, there are equal problems. It implies that there is an
independent standard of good, known to human reason, by which
you can judge God's action and therefore declare it to be 'good'.
But this is to create an authority over and above God, which is
what the religious person will not accept.

Key thought

It is possible to use this dilemma
as a basis for arguing for a natural
law approach to ethics. In other
words, if God is the rational
creator of everything, then the
universe should display a rational
structure and purpose. Human
reason, in contemplating the
universe, is thus (whether it
recognises it or not) also
contemplating God.

4 Ethics and the religious traditions

In order to appreciate the moral arguments presented from within a
religious tradition, it is necessary to get some idea of the basis and
authority upon which such arguments are founded – whether, for
example, they are based on a 'divine command' theory, or on the
authority of a sacred text, or priesthood, or whether they are
justified with reference to human reason.

Judaism

Fundamental to Jewish ethics is the *Torah*, with the addition of the
Mishna (oral traditions, believed to have been given to Moses by God)
and its commentary, the *Gemara*. Together these form the *Talmud*, an
encyclopaedia of rules and traditions, governing every aspect of life.

- The moral authority of this tradition is seen as divine in origin, but as subject to interpretation and application to particular situations.
- It is clearly deontological, rather than utilitarian or teleological, since it is a systematic interpretation of duties towards God and towards other people. In general, obedience takes precedence over anticipated results.
- Human reason is a vehicle for interpretation, but not – as in Kant – a primary source of morality. Interpretation builds up a body of tradition, and following tradition is important chiefly as an expression of loyalty and obedience.
- Reason itself is seen as embodied in the voice of God, 'calling' creation into existence. In this sense, there may be parallels with a natural law approach, since humankind is to align itself with the will of a rational creator God. The *Torah* is seen as a fundamental element in creation, rather than being merely words.

Christianity

The ultimate authority for Christian morality is God's will. But that will, it is believed, is known through the medium of Jesus' life and teachings, as recorded in the New Testament, passed on through the teachings of the Church and revealed through the inspiration of the Holy Spirit.

Christians have not always agreed about how these three should be balanced. For example, at the Reformation, the reformers shifted away from using the authority of the Church, towards the authority of scriptures as interpreted by each individual. On the other hand, of course, scholars will readily point out that the scriptures are not divine edicts handed down verbatim, but are themselves part of the process of interpretation and tradition within the early Church. Hence, the debate may come down to the authority of a particular interpretation, rather than the authority of the scriptures themselves.

Key thought

For Christianity, there are three vehicles by which the ultimate source of authority is known: scriptures, tradition and inspiration.

- Christian morality depends on an interpretation of God's will, rather than on unaided human reason.
- The process of balancing early interpretations of scripture with contemporary ones may well depend upon a believer's idea of the authority given to the present-day Church by the inspiration of the Holy Spirit.
- Beyond all this there is the belief that what was revealed in Christ was actually the agent of creation (the *logos*), a rational principle behind the universe, a concept that had already been explored by the Stoics, and parallels the creative role of the *Torah* in Judaism. Hence there is the sense (as revealed in the 'natural law' approach) that reason and revelation should complement rather than oppose one another.

- Historically, Christianity, in separating itself from Judaism, defined its moral stance in contrast to what it portrayed as the legalism of its parent religion. Hence the emphasis on the demands of love rather than obedience to tradition, as seen for example in situation ethics.
- Christianity has always regarded the conscience of the individual as a vehicle of moral insight. In this case, conscience is not an alternative source of moral authority, but depends on the belief that the conscience is given by God.

Islam

The authorities for Muslim ethics are the *Qur'an* and the *Hadith* of the Prophet Muhammad. As with Judaism and Christianity, Islam recognises that interpretation is necessary in order to apply these to present-day issues. An authoritative ruling is given by a meeting of recognised Muslim scholars (the *ulama*).

There is also the fundamental belief that Muslims are those who 'submit' to the Will of Allah, and that to do so is to live in a natural way, at one with Him as the creative source of all things. Such natural living is referred to as the *Shariah* (which may be translated as 'path').

Key thoughts

Since Islam and Shariah are natural, every child is considered to be born Muslim, even if, through the circumstances of their birth, culture or conviction, they subsequently turn away from Islam.

When Muslim law is applied, individual circumstances are taken into account. To be morally responsible, a person must be an adult of sound mind, must not be coerced into the act in question, and must not act out of desperation.

- Scriptures, interpreted by appropriate authority, are basic to Muslim ethics.
- There are parallels to the natural law approach to ethics, since Allah – as creator – wants everyone to 'submit' and live in a natural way.
- Muslim ethics is clearly deontological rather than consequentialist: duty in obeying the Will of Allah is paramount.
- Islam accepts a valid role for human reason, but does not regard it as in any way an independent source of authority for matters of religion and ethics.

Hinduism

Hindu ethics reflect the wide range of traditions and cultures, along with the beliefs and spiritual practices that sustain them. In considering ethical issues within the Hindu traditions, it is important to distinguish between those things that are grounded in fundamental religious beliefs and those that are the product of social traditions.

- The Vedic term *Dharma* refers to the 'duty' of individuals to follow the natural order of things, as well as the creative principle that gives rise to such order. Hindu ethics may therefore be seen as deontological, with natural law elements.
- One's dharma is socially defined, and also depends upon one's stage in life. Judgement about particular actions is therefore relativist (or, more accurately, situationist) rather than absolute.

Key thought

Ethical action is seen as a spiritual practice in itself (*karma marga*), leading the individual towards liberation.

- The recognition of social differences and expectations (influenced by belief in *karma* – the idea that one's actions have consequences in this or a future life) is very different from the assumption made, for example, by utilitarianism that all people should be treated equally and have an equal share in the anticipated benefits of an action.
- Unlike the Western tendency to examine ethics primarily from the standpoint of individual choice, Hindu morality emphasises its social implications: a person's actions take on significance and value depending on his or her position in society and its corresponding duties.

Buddhism

There are fundamental differences between Buddhist ethics and those of the other religions we are considering in this chapter. These stem from the fact that Buddhism is not based on acceptance of, or commitment to, a fixed set of beliefs. Rather, it is a philosophy which invites each individual to explore the nature of reality, and to reach his or her own personal conviction.

- Although the teachings of Gautama and the scriptures within which they are preserved are treated with great respect, the fact that each Buddhist is required to examine and evaluate them before accepting them, implies that reason takes priority over scriptures and tradition. This applies to ethical principles as to all other propositions.
- Recognising that each individual is unique, some Buddhist traditions place emphasis on individual guidance from a teacher in matters of spiritual development, which include morality.
- Buddhists tend to speak of actions as *kushala* (skilful) or *akushala* (unskilful) depending on whether they stem from compassion, generosity and wisdom, or from hatred, craving and delusion.
- As in virtue ethics (see p.150), Buddhism sees action as arising as a result of personal character traits, which are themselves formed as a result of earlier actions.
- The doctrine of *karma*, which Buddhism took from the Hindu traditions within which it arose, does not totally determine actions or circumstances, but is one factor to be taken into account. In other words, everything arises dependent upon conditions, and one's *karma* (the results of ethically significant actions in the past) forms one of those conditions.
- At a basic, or conventional level, lay Buddhists accept five precepts: not to destroy life; not to steal; not to indulge in harmful sexual activity, or to indulge the senses; not to speak falsely, or to deceive; not to cloud the mind with intoxicants. These are accepted as 'rules for training', in other words they are 'hypothetical' rather than 'categorical' imperatives. In effect, they

say 'If you wish to make progress along the Buddhist path of wisdom and compassion, then you should adopt these as principles to guide you.' There is no divine lawgiver in Buddhism. Buddhists ethics are also shaped by the desire to cultivate four mental states: love; pity; joy; serenity.

- The process of training appears to be similar to that of modern virtue ethics. However, whereas virtue ethics looks to human flourishing as its ultimate criterion of what is good, Buddhist ethics has a goal that goes beyond any benefit to the individual self. Indeed, the idea of a goal of human flourishing would, for a Buddhist, be seen as a sign of self-centredness, and therefore be a sign of delusion.
- The goal, for Buddhists, is an awareness of the interconnected nature of all things, and to live in a way that reflects that awareness. It is therefore very different from a natural law approach, which seeks to understand the 'end' or goal of individual entities.

Sikhism

The Sikh religion has always placed emphasis on equality. This not only contrasted with the Hindu caste system, but also sought to overcome the wider distinction between Muslims and Hindus (itself a major issue at the time when it was founded). This is demonstrated in the Sikh requirement that all worshippers should be prepared to sit and eat together.

- The fundamental authority for Sikhs is the Will of God, as embodied in the teachings of the ten Gurus and the *Guru Granth Sahib*, their holy book. As with other religions, there is the need to decide on an authoritative interpretation, and this has led to the acceptance of the *Rehat Maryada*, a guide to the Sikh way of life, produced in 1945 by a group of Sikh scholars.
- The Sikh emphasis on equality may be paralleled with Kant's second form of the categorical imperative, in that every individual is to be treated as an 'end' in himself or herself. However, the basis of this equality is very different, since Kant's is derived solely from human reason.
- There are parallels between Sikh ethics and virtue ethics, since Sikhs believe that people are naturally prone to live in a state of illusion, dominated by five evil impulses: lust; anger; greed; attachment to worldly things; pride. They are therefore encouraged to cultivate their opposites: self-control; forgiveness; contentment; love of God; humility. Notice however the ultimate justification of cultivating these virtues. Whereas for modern virtue ethics the aim is human flourishing, requiring no religious underpinning, for Sikhs it is based entirely on the desire to follow the Will of God.

Key thought

Buddhist ethics is largely situationist, in that it recognises that individual circumstances, rather than general rules, determine the nature of skilful action.

Key thought

Sikh ethics are mainly deontological, since they are concerned with the duties of individuals. Even if a utilitarian argument might justify the Sikh position on ethical issues, for Sikhs the issue of right and wrong is given by God, through the inspiration of the Gurus, and is not a matter of assessing results.

Since this book is concerned with ethical theory, we have not examined the actual moral practices of religious believers. For that, students need to refer to books on whichever religion they are studying.

The crucial thing to recognise, however, is the source of authority and the method or argument used by a religious person in coming to a moral decision. His or her conclusions about what is right might be identical to those of someone from another religion, or someone arguing from a purely secular or rational point of view. It is not the conclusions that distinguish religious and secular ethics, but *the way in which those conclusions are reached, and subsequent actions are justified.*

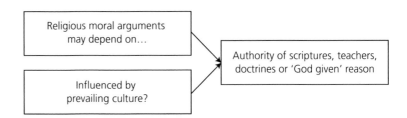

Study guide

By the end of this chapter you should recognise the mutual influence of religion and society, and be able to assess the degree to which a moral argument is autonomous, or dependent on religious beliefs or sources of authority.

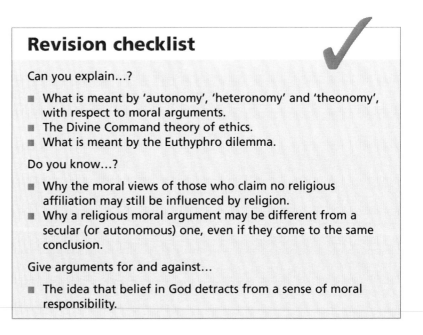

Revision checklist

Can you explain...?

- What is meant by 'autonomy', 'heteronomy' and 'theonomy', with respect to moral arguments.
- The Divine Command theory of ethics.
- What is meant by the Euthyphro dilemma.

Do you know...?

- Why the moral views of those who claim no religious affiliation may still be influenced by religion.
- Why a religious moral argument may be different from a secular (or autonomous) one, even if they come to the same conclusion.

Give arguments for and against...

- The idea that belief in God detracts from a sense of moral responsibility.

Example of essay question

1. Religious ethics is necessarily deontological. Discuss with reference to the perspectives of the religion you have studied.

AO1 requires a clear statement of what is meant by 'deontological', contrasting using duty as a starting point with other theories, such as utilitarianism.

AO2 involves a discussion of whether religion implies 'duty'. So, for example, one might ask if Christian situation ethics is at least partly utilitarian in its approach, or whether natural law ethics implies that the right thing is that which leads to a natural fulfilment of your human potential. One could use Kant's view of the disinterested performance of one's duty, and discuss whether this is reflected in the religion you have studied.

Further questions

1 It is inappropriate to apply Jesus' moral teaching to those who are not members of the Christian religion. Discuss.

2 Ethics can never be completely separated from religion. Discuss.

CONSCIENCE

Chapter checklist ✓

The term 'conscience' may be used in both secular and religious moral arguments, and refers to an inner conviction about what is right or wrong. The main issues we shall be considering in this chapter are the origin of conscience, its validity as a source of moral authority, and its place within a moral argument.

1 A Christian view

Key word

Syneidesis: the New Testament term for conscience. Negatively, it refers to the pain suffered by one who goes against his or her moral principles, and positively to having a 'good conscience' before God.

In Romans 2:15, conscience is described as the witness to the 'requirements of the law', written on the heart of those who are not under the law – in other words, conscience acts as a moral guide, even for those people who do not consciously take into consideration specific moral principles or rules. It is also interesting to note from the same epistle (1:18ff) that the wrath of God is described as being revealed from heaven against those who go against his moral laws, and the justification for such wrath is there is no excuse or plea of ignorance, since God's invisible qualities of eternal power and divine nature have been revealed in creation. The implication here is that everyone has a conscience which can respond, even if unconsciously, to the requirements of the divine law. In a sense, this presents conscience as part of a 'natural law' theory, in that the recognition of basic religious and moral principles is built into the structure of the universe and human nature.

Thus, within Christian moral teaching, conscience is regarded as the voice of God within the soul. This is how it is expressed by Schleiermacher, writing in 1830:

We use the term 'conscience' to express the fact that all modes of activity issuing from our God-consciousness and subject to its prompting confront us as moral demands, not indeed theoretically, but asserting themselves in our self-consciousness in such a way that any deviation of

Key people

Friedrich Schleiermacher (1768–1834)
was a Protestant theologian and Professor of Philosophy and Theology at the University of Berlin. Schleiermacher wanted to reinstate the significance of the academic study of religion, following the rationalist critiques of the Enlightenment period. See particularly his *On Religion: speeches to its cultured despisers* (1799).

our conduct from them is apprehended as a hindrance to life, and therefore as sin. … conscience also is very markedly traced to divine causality, and, as the voice of God within, is held to be an original revelation of God; it is one of those inward experiences which we may assume to be universal in this sphere.

(*The Christian Faith*, Chapter 83)

In other words, Schleiermacher links conscience directly to a person's awareness of God, so that going against one's conscience is seen as sin. The implication here is that conscience is the product of revelation rather than reason. Although reason may subsequently justify moral actions that have been prompted by conscience, that prompting itself comes from God.

2 The secular conscience

In a secular context, conscience depends on two things:

- freedom
- knowledge of the good.

Without freedom, conscience makes no sense. It is not logical to have an inner conviction that you ought to do something that is impossible. But equally, conscience implies some innate knowledge of 'the good'. Without that, conscience could prompt no specific action.

a) The origin of conscience

From the religious standpoint, conscience is the voice of God. But what other explanations can be given for this innate sense of right and wrong?

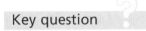

Key question

Does our conscience simply reflect what society has taught us?

- One possibility is that all our moral views are *socially and culturally conditioned*. Thus, for example, Hegel spoke of the 'spirit' of each age, which determined moral as well as cultural and aesthetic awareness. This suggests that we judge what we should do in terms of the values that are held by the society within which we live. If, for example, we are utilitarian, we will want to do that which offers the greatest happiness for the greatest number of people, but the *nature* of that 'happiness' or benefit will come from values given to us by the society within which we live. If social values have become embedded in our unconscious mind, we may experience them as the promptings of conscience.

- Another possibility, closely related to the first, is that our conscience, and particularly our sense of guilt, can be explained in *psychological* terms. During our early upbringing, we take on certain values and ideas which – even if consciously rejected at a later stage in life – continue to influence our moral awareness through the promptings of our conscience. Freud made the distinction between the *ego*, *id* and *super-ego*. In the simplest of terms, the first of these is the rational self, the second represents the self at the level of its physical and emotional needs, and the third is the controlling self, imposing rules on what the ego, prompted by the needs of the id, can do. Conscience, in this scheme, would be an aspect of the operation of the super-ego. A Freudian approach would therefore see the conscience as a product of the rules that we were taught by our parents, or other adults, in childhood.

A combination of both social and psychological factors influenced the work of Piaget, who examined the stages of child development. He thought that before the age of ten, children generally took their moral awareness from parents and others around them. After that age, they were able to develop their own set of moral principles, and have an increasing awareness of the purpose and social function of morality. This approach saw the development of conscience as natural, but as influenced by external factors.

The further possibility is that we have *an innate sense of right and wrong*, which does not depend on our early experiences or later conditioning. This is suggested by the fact that conscience is almost a universal phenomenon. The exception is the *psychopath*: the person who has no moral sense or feeling. The psychopath may be extremely intelligent, socially manipulative or charming, but has no awareness of other people as people, or any sense that their wishes or needs should be taken into account. Now psychopathology is a complex science, and we can offer no more than a caricature here, but the assumption remains that 'normal' people have some innate sense of right and wrong and of what is acceptable behaviour. This is shown by the fact that they have a conscience and can show remorse when they have done something wrong.

One way to see the significance of this is to look at the 'normal' development of moral awareness. In *The Philosophy of Moral Development*, 1981, Lawrence Kohlberg set out six stages of development:

- obedience for fear of punishment
- decisions made on the basis of self-interest
- decisions made with a sense of what is expected of you
- obedience of rules because they are important for the society of which we are a member.

But it is when we come to his final two stages that we encounter the sort of ethical theory that we have been considering so far:

- a utilitarian concern for others, or the sense of a social contract
- an awareness of 'universal ethical principles' and respect for individuals.

Key people

Jean Piaget (1896–1980)
was a Swiss psychologist and philosopher, known particularly for his work on the development of learning in children. He was influential in promoting child-centred learning, and concerned that children should grow to be creative rather than conformist.

Key people

Lawrence Kohlberg (1927–87)
became involved in moral questions while helping to smuggle Jews through a Palestine blockade during the Second World War. Subsequently he studied the process of moral decision-making at the University of Chicago. He did research work on Piaget's theory of development, and spent the last twenty years of his life as Professor of Education and Social Psychology at Yale.

As we go through that process, it is clear that the conscience seems to operate at the fifth and sixth stages. However, Kohlberg argues that we can only reach these higher stages having passed through the earlier ones. This leaves us with the question of whether the earlier stages – in which fear, self-interest, or the need to conform to expectations play an important part – are actually the formative source of the developing conscience.

b) Conscience as a source of moral authority

In Chapter 8 we examined some of the sources of moral authority. We noted that Rousseau held that there were two primitive emotions, one of which was a natural repugnance at the sufferings of others. He believed that this moral sense was innate, and was only masked by social convention. Similarly Frances Hutcheson believed that people had a natural sense of benevolence, and that this – rather than reason – was the source of morality.

Bishop Butler considered that there was a hierarchy of authority within the self, with conscience at the top, superior to the appetites and passions. In particular, he considered that the conscience was able to overcome an instinctive concern for the self, and enable people to consider the welfare of others. He thought that everyone had a conscience, and that to know what was right it was only necessary to give attention to it – to listen to the 'guide within'. As a Christian, he believed that God had designed the human personality to be controlled by its conscience and that to follow one's conscience was therefore to act in accordance with nature.

Butler thought that conscience gave an intuitive awareness of right and wrong; it did not involve any form of calculation. He held that conscience had its own authority. Therefore some things – for example lies or unprovoked violence – are wrong, quite apart from any calculation of the happiness or misery that may result from them.

He believed that God created humans in such a way that their good will come from obeying the conscience that God has provided for their guidance. We should follow it because it is the law of our own nature (in that it indicates the naturalness or unnaturalness of actions) and virtue consists in following nature.

Thus, Butler's role for the conscience is one that sorts out competing claims of affections and emotions, enabling us to act with integrity. Just as Plato (see p.48) argued that reason should rule over the spirited elements and appetites in humankind, Butler argued that the role is taken by the conscience. It is conscience that leads to moral dilemmas and therefore to rational discussions of right and wrong, but conscience takes priority and initiates them.

One criticism of Butler, made by Elizabeth Anscombe (in 'Modern Moral Philosophy', *Philosophy*, 1958), is that Butler does not take into account that, in the name of conscience, people may do the vilest

Key people

Joseph Butler (1692–1752) was Bishop of Durham. He took a position on ethics that was midway between Hutcheson's 'moral sense' view based on emotions and one based on reason. In particular, he saw the conscience as acting to balance a natural self-love against benevolence towards others.

Key thought

This means that, in the long run, conscience is not going to run counter to a natural sense of self-love, since it will serve one's own good.

things. Butler assumes that conscience, having been given by God in order to direct the self, will always be good. He does not consider that it may be distorted or evil. This raises a fundamental question: How do you decide between two conflicting consciences?

G. E. Moore, in claiming that 'good' could not be defined, nevertheless insisted that people knew what it meant – and that, of course, implies some innate sense or intuition. If conscience gives us an innate sense of right and wrong, this takes priority over logical arguments that are used to justify moral choice. In this sense, conscience becomes the starting point of morality, for without a sense of right and wrong, moral issues and arguments would never arise.

Conscience is also related to the idea of *integrity*. If we do one thing whilst believing that we should really be doing another, our conscience may trouble us, reminding us of our loss of integrity. *Integrity implies a good conscience.* Insofar as personal integrity is seen as a valid goal for human life, it adds to the significance and authority of conscience.

However, we need to take care to make sure that what we think of as a voice of conscience is not simply the result of fear of going against a socially ingrained rule. The psychologist Erich Fromm put it this way:

> *In most social systems, obedience is the supreme virtue, disobedience the supreme sin. When most people feel 'guilty', they are actually feeling afraid because they have been disobedient. They are not really troubled by a moral issue, as they think they are, but by the fact of having disobeyed a command.*
>
> *(quoted in a review of* On Disobedience and Other Essays, *1984)*

Fromm was particularly concerned with the issue of freedom and the extent to which society encourages us to obey, making us feel guilty if we do not.

c) The conscience and moral arguments

A moral argument is the rational examination of issues of right and wrong. Take, for example, utilitarianism. On the principle of utility – seeking the greatest happiness (or benefit) for the greatest number – it assesses a situation and makes a calculation about how happiness might be maximised. But that does not in itself define what is good, it merely organises how what we already know to be good might best be brought about. This was why G. E. Moore insisted that it needed to be supplemented (as the utilitarian Sidgwick had done) by a basic intuition of 'good'. Without some such intuition, it fell into the trap of trying to argue for an 'ought' on the basis of an 'is'.

If we look at the natural law approach to ethics – where ideas of right and wrong are related to the end or purpose for which something has been created – we find that Aquinas (in *Summa*

Key people

Erich Fromm (1900–80)
Having first studied law and sociology, Fromm became interested in psychology and completed his training as a psychoanalyst, before escaping from an increasingly Nazi-dominated Germany, first to Switzerland and then to the United States. He spent the last years of his life in Switzerland, and continued to work as a clinical psychologist, having established a huge international reputation through his many books.

Key thought

Although conscience is not infallible, Aquinas still considered it to be authoritative.

Key people

John Henry Newman (1801–90)
As an Anglican priest, Newman was convinced that the Anglican Church should return to its roots in Catholic doctrine and liturgical practice. Eventually he was converted to Catholicism and received into the Catholic Church in 1845, going on to become a Cardinal.

Key question

Is it ever right for one's conscience to overrule one's rationally argued ethical position?

Theologiae) claimed that there are in fact *two* ways to act badly: one is to do what is known to be wrong, and the other is to go against one's own conscience. For Aquinas the conscience was the natural ability, given to humankind by God, to understand and apply moral principles. It could be mistaken, however, if the person either misunderstood or was ignorant of a moral rule, or if he or she did not realise that the rule should apply to their particular situation.

Even though it may be authoritative, notice that conscience is not independent of a basic understanding of the nature of reality – as created by God, for example, and as having a natural 'end' or purpose. Thus, *conscience is more like a skill than a body of knowledge*; it is the natural and intuitive skill of being able to understand and apply moral principles.

Clearly, for Christian theologians, the idea of conscience is closely linked to that of God as creator. Newman followed Aquinas in seeing conscience as the ability to appreciate and apply moral principles, but he was closer to Bishop Butler in seeing it as intuitive, rather than rational. Its function was to stimulate and inform the process of moral decision-making. The feelings associated with conscience – guilt or shame, for example – are those of men and women who recognise that they are responsible to God (as ruler and judge) for their actions.

It could be argued that conscience should inform the process of rational ethical thought, but it should not take priority. Butler and others would claim that conscience is superior, while those who see it as socially acquired may well consider it less important than reason for deciding ethical matters.

In general, therefore, we see that conscience, or the innate knowledge of right and wrong, is not only compatible with moral arguments, but is seen as lying behind them. It is because we have a conscience that it makes sense to engage in moral arguments.

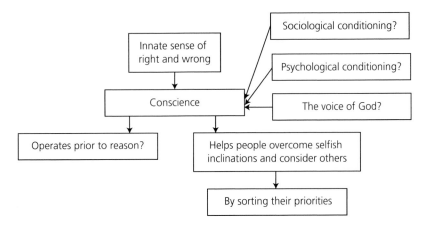

Study guide

By the end of this chapter you should understand the Christian and secular ideas of conscience, and be aware of the possible sources of conscience in social and psychological conditioning, the nature of the authority that the conscience has, and the way in which it relates to rational arguments about moral issues.

Revision checklist ✓

Can you explain...?

- Why conscience implies an innate knowledge of 'the good'.
- Why some claim that the conscience is socially or psychologically conditioned.
- Why Butler, Newman and others have argued that conscience is intuitive rather than rational.

Do you know...?

- Why Butler claimed that conscience did not involve any form of calculation.
- Why a psychopath illustrates the function of the conscience.

Give arguments for and against...

- The view that conscience is the product of upbringing or environment.

Examples of essay questions

1. Whatever the situation in law, a person is generally considered to be morally guilty or innocent not just because of what he or she has done, but why. Discuss the role of motive and personal integrity in assessing moral praise or blame, with special reference to the role of conscience.

For AO1, relevant knowledge here might include the sense in which natural law (and virtue ethics, for those who have already studied this) is concerned with integrity of the personality, in the sense of fulfilling its 'end'. Motive could also be considered with reference to utilitarianism – as to whether something is right, if the results are positive, even if done for the wrong motive.

AO2 requires a view about the extent to which conscience is innate and implies personal integrity.

2. Is conscience a necessary part of an ethical view of life? Discuss.

For AO1, in answering this question, it might be worth reflecting on those ethical theories – e.g. utilitarianism – which seem to give a method of assessing right from wrong that does not require a direct reference to motive or conscience. Higher level answers might focus on the importance of specifying what is 'necessary' in order to have a moral discussion.

The key focus for AO2 here is the word 'necessary'. Nobody is likely to argue that they have no part to play, but only whether it is a sufficient and necessary prerequisite for a moral claim.

Further questions

1 'Conscience is the voice of God.' Explain why some might claim this. To what extent do you agree with this view of conscience?

2 Is the statement 'You should always follow your conscience' acceptable?

16 VIRTUE ETHICS

Chapter checklist ✓

In this chapter we shall look at modern virtue ethics, its origins in Aristotle, its relationship to natural law, and its particular relevance for feminist thought.

1 Background

Three ethical theories have dominated Western thinking over the last two hundred years or so:

- Natural law
- Kant's deontological approach
- Utilitarianism.

The first and oldest of these, associated particularly with Catholic thinking and heavily coloured by Aquinas' use of Aristotle, roots its approach to ethics in the view that every act or thing has an 'essence' – that which makes it what it is and gives it a place and meaning within the universe – an essence given to it by a creator God. In secular debate, however, the arguments have mostly polarised into those based on pure reason, stemming from Kant, and utilitarian arguments based on the anticipated results of an action.

There is, however, another strand of ethical thinking which goes back to the work of Aristotle, and which is closely linked to the natural law approach: virtue ethics. This was a key feature of Aristotle's ethics, and depends – as does the natural law tradition – on an understanding of the essence or fundamental nature of things.

Virtues are those qualities that enable human beings to express their true nature. Looked at in this way, it is clear that virtue ethics is really an extension of the natural law approach. However, it is an aspect of that approach which was largely neglected until its revival in the middle of the twentieth century.

Key question ?

Virtue ethics starts with the basic question: 'What does it mean to live a good life?'

Today, virtue ethics stands as an ethical theory in its own right, and not merely as an extension to natural law. In a secular context, it examines those qualities which lead to human flourishing, and does so in a way that is quite distinct from other ethical theories, and has been found to be particularly appropriate in considering women's issues and concerns.

2 What are the virtues?

Key quote

'It is not correct to speak of modesty as a kind of virtue, because it is more like a feeling than a state. It is defined … as a sort of fear of disrepute, and it has an effect very like that produced by the fear of danger … We consider that adolescents ought to be modest because, living as they do under the sway of their feelings, they often make mistakes, but are restrained by modesty. Also we commend a modest youth, but nobody would commend an older man for being shamefaced, because we think that he ought not to do anything to be ashamed of.'

ARISTOTLE, *ETHICS*, BOOK 4, X

Key thought

Both the natural law approach and virtue ethics are based on a fundamental understanding of the nature of humankind, and therefore of what constitutes the 'good life' for human beings. They may be seen as two aspects of a single argument.

Key thought

This is the distinctive feature of virtue ethics; it examines those qualities which make for the 'good life'.

What counts as a virtue depends very much upon circumstances. Thus, for a military person, courage would be a key virtue. For a religious person, humility and obedience might be equally important. From a humanist standpoint, prudence and self-control might be key features of the 'good life'. Socially, one might consider modesty, politeness or being good-humoured as virtues.

Plato, Aristotle and the Stoics considered that there were four 'cardinal' virtues (from *cardo*, meaning a hinge) which formed the basis of the moral life. They are:

- temperance (or moderation)
- justice
- courage
- prudence (or wisdom).

The exercise of these was considered to lead to a life 'in full', expressing the essence of humankind. There are many other virtues, some related to religion (e.g. the Christian virtue of humility), others to social function. But all share the quality of being character traits, or dispositions, to act in ways that allow people to live well.

There is a large measure of agreement between ethical theories on what sorts of action may be considered good. What distinguishes one theory from another is the way in which the argument is presented, and the criteria by which actions are judged. What is clear is that a Kantian may argue in favour of telling the truth, but will do so on the grounds that dishonesty will ultimately be self-defeating, and will destroy the very nature of the concept of truth. Equally, a utilitarian may argue for honesty, but only because it will, in the end, lead to the greatest happiness of the greatest number. The different between these and a virtue ethics approach is that the virtue ethicist seeks to promote honesty in its own right because human flourishing requires the cultivation of the virtues, of which honesty is one.

Aristotle held that the only worthwhile thing in life was to cultivate the virtues – that is what 'being good' is all about. And that fits in with our usual way of speaking. If I describe someone as 'good', I do not necessarily refer to a particular action that I consider to be right, but rather that this person shows a quality, a disposition, a habit to behave in a way that I call 'good'. In other words, to describe people as 'good' is as much a description of the way they 'are' as a description of what they actually 'do'.

3 Virtue ethics in Aristotle

In the *Nicomachean Ethics*, Aristotle is concerned to show that virtue is its own reward, and does not need to be justified in terms of some other benefit:

> … *lovers of beauty find pleasure in things that are pleasant by nature, and virtuous actions are of this kind, so that they are pleasant not only to this type of person but also in themselves. So their life does not need to have pleasure attached to it as a sort of accessory, but contains its own pleasure in itself. Indeed we may go further and assert that anyone who does not delight in fine actions is not even a good man; for nobody would say that a man is just unless he enjoys acting justly, nor liberal unless he enjoys liberal actions, and similarly in all the other cases. If this is so, virtuous actions must be pleasurable in themselves.*

Key thought

For Aristotle, happiness is not simply given, it requires an active and thoughtful engagement with life.

As we saw in Chapter 6, Aristotle saw 'happiness' (*eudaimonia*) as the goal in life, something which was sought for itself rather than as a means to some other end. And this happiness consisted as much in living the good life, as in enjoying the good things of life.

Hence he regarded the virtues as qualities that are to be cultivated, expressed through and reinforced by action. They are more like a habit to be acquired, than a chance description of a single action. They also express the mean between extremes (see page 56). The classic example of this is his claim that *courage* is a virtue that represents the mean between, on the one hand *cowardice* (a deficiency) and *rashness* (an excess). It does not represent an average of people's behaviour, but a balance between two tendencies that could prove equally damaging.

Key thought

The 'good life', for Stoics, was one that displayed the virtues that came from living in a way that reflected the *logos* of the universe.

Aristotle's views were taken up by the Stoics (see page 58). They thought that the quest for virtue, rather than happiness, would enable the individual to act in a way that brought him or her into line with the overall rational purpose that directed everything.

4 The revival of virtue ethics

It is generally considered that a significant factor in the modern revival of virtue ethics was the publication of an article entitled 'Modern Moral Philosophy' by Elizabeth Anscombe in 1958.

- She argued that, since many did not believe in God, it was important to find a system of morality that could be based on the

Key people

**Elizabeth Anscombe
(1919–2001)**
was probably best known for her work in developing modern virtue ethics. She was influenced by Wittgenstein, who had been her teacher at Cambridge (where she later became a professor), and she was instrumental in preparing his later work for publication. Her ethical writings show the influence of her Catholicism, particularly in her opposition to abortion. It was Anscombe who coined the term 'consequentialism' for those ethical theories (developed from earlier utilitarianism) which considered both intended and unintended consequences of an action in assessing its moral significance.

idea of human flourishing – living the 'good life' – rather than obedience to the rules of an external lawgiver.

- She argued that Kant's idea that reason would provide a self-regulating system of morality (in other words, that we would recognise and respond to the demands of the categorical imperative) was not a sensible one, and that most traditional moral arguments – particularly Kantian ethics and utilitarianism – required some idea of an external lawgiver to support them.
- She highlighted the fact that in most ethical theories the term 'ought' is the equivalent of 'is obliged to', and this implies that there is a law and thus a lawgiver.

The result of Anscombe's challenge to traditional ethical theories was a re-examination of Aristotle's idea of the virtues as a basis for a modern secular form of ethics. Going back to Aristotle, and thus to a pre-Christian ethics, we find that he used 'ought' in a rather different sense – as in (to use Anscombe's own example) you 'ought' to oil a machine if it is to work properly. It is not that there is an external law to be applied, but simply that a machine needs oil if it is to function properly.

Virtue ethics therefore asks what is implied by saying that someone is 'good' or 'generous' or 'courageous'. It is asking about qualities and dispositions to act, rather than looking – in a legalistic fashion – at the possible rights or wrongs of particular actions.

One of the most influential books on modern virtue ethics is Alasdair MacIntyre's *After Virtue* (1981). In it, he defines a virtue thus:

A virtue is an acquired human quality the possession of and exercise of which tends to enable us to achieve those goods which are internal to practices and the lack of which effectively prevents us from achieving any such goods.

(page 178)

This is best understood by taking a simple example. Suppose I want to succeed as an artist. I might try to achieve fame by cheating, or assume that I can produce something brilliant without effort. But even if I fooled some people by doing that, I would not actually become a good artist. In order genuinely to achieve my goal, I would need to exercise the virtues of justice and honesty in producing and displaying my work; I would also need courage and determination to stretch and develop my skills.

Notice also that MacIntyre says that a virtue is 'acquired'. It is not simply a matter of being born with certain qualities, but of working to develop and exercise them. If ethics is based on developing the virtues, it is open to everyone to try to do so, not limited to those who happen to find it easy or who are naturally inclined to develop them.

Key thought

The virtues are what will enable me to achieve the good that is inherent in what I have chosen to do.

Key thought

Humility may be seen as a key Christian quality, but for Aristotle or Homer it would more likely have been considered a vice. Remember Nietzsche's 'slave morality' and 'master morality'? Virtues are selected to fit goals.

MacIntyre considers three different concepts of 'virtue', from three different periods:

- In Homer, virtue is what enables someone to discharge their social obligations. Courage, for example, is the key requirement of the warrior.
- In Aristotle, the virtues enable a person to move towards a natural or supernatural 'end' or goal in life.
- In the eighteenth century, Benjamin Franklin lists virtues as qualities that enable one to be successful.

Not only do each of these depend on some prior understanding of the goal of life, but each version of that goal will determine what qualities are seen as virtues.

Another approach to the virtues, taken by Philippa Foot (in *Virtue Ethics*, 1977) is to see them as correcting existing human tendencies. Thus, for example, there is a natural human tendency to self-interest, which needs to be corrected by the virtue of benevolence. Foot also made the distinction between the moral hero, who has to struggle to do what is right, and the moral saint, who naturally does what is right. She holds that the saint is superior, although the hero has the greater power of will. Notice how different this is from Kant's view. For Kant, to act out of natural inclination or disposition, rather than from a conviction of moral duty, is morally neutral. For him, it is only the heroic that counts – for the saint, being naturally good, moral principles are irrelevant.

5 Feminist ethics

Feminist ideas are associated particularly with social and political thinking, since they emphasise the way in which a male-orientated society has disadvantaged women, but they are also relevant to ethics. By looking at ethical issues from a woman's point of view, feminist ethics seeks to restore the balance in what it sees as a male-dominated way of examining moral issues, and thus work towards ethical perspectives that are equally applicable to men and women.

Virtue ethics was particularly attractive to feminist thinkers, since they felt that the traditional moral arguments, based on ideas of duty and rights, were the product of a male way of looking at moral issues, and that they did not give adequate account of qualities – such as care and compassion – that had important implications for ethical issues, but which were also seen as particularly relevant to the experience and concerns of women. In particular, much traditional ethics has been concerned with individual personal autonomy, which feminists see as a distinctively male trait, as opposed to a female emphasis on relationships and mutual support.

One key question for virtue ethics, especially in a feminist context, is whether or not we have a fixed 'essence' or are mainly the product of social or psychological conditioning. This was highlighted by Simone de Beauvoir, who in her influential book *The Second Sex* (1949) raised the issue of whether one was born a woman, or becomes a woman – in other words, whether those things that we associate with the feminine are natural or a social construction. If the latter, they may well have been imposed on women (and sometimes unconsciously accepted by them) by a male-dominated society.

Virtue ethics has particular value for feminist thought in that it invites a consideration of those qualities that lead to human flourishing (thus applicable equally to men and women), rather than concentrating on the traditional ethical arguments, which appeared to be underpinned by belief in a divine, male lawgiver.

Key quote

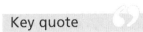

'One is not born, but rather becomes, a woman.'

SIMONE DE BEAUVOIR

6 The distinctiveness of virtue ethics

Notice that, whereas other ethical theories tend to focus on the right or wrong of particular acts, virtue ethics is more concerned with the cultivation of qualities which express themselves in actions, but are not simply to be identified with them.

Iris Murdoch, in *The Sovereignty of Good* (2001), pointed out that we act at any given moment on the basis of those habitual ways of understanding the world and responding to it that we have built up over a long period of time. In doing what we do, we are unlikely to act completely out of character, but will have been trained by our life experience to respond to a situation in one way or another. Hence the crucial fact that virtue ethics considers the development of those virtues, the exercise of which will be good for human flourishing. They may suggest particular actions in particular situations, but cannot prescribe them.

Notice that some virtues – for example, courage, temperance and wisdom – are likely to be of immediate benefit to the person who possesses them, quite apart from the effect that they have on others. A virtue such as charity, for example, is directed out towards others. If being courageous is of benefit to me, it makes no sense to ask why I should bother to be courageous – as though it were something commanded from outside. If it is to my benefit, it is naturally something to be desired. The matter is less clear with a virtue that relates to others, and therefore it makes more sense to ask 'Why should I bother to be charitable?' In such cases, those who take a virtue ethics approach are likely to bring into consideration issues such as the will (I do something because I choose to do it, irrespective of any immediate benefit to myself), or

Key people

Iris Murdoch (1919–99)
Although best known as a novelist, Iris Murdoch was also a philosopher. She was particularly interested in existentialism and in ethics. As well as *The Sovereignty of Good*, her most immediately relevant book for those studying ethics is *Metaphysics as a Guide to Morals*.

else they relate it to a general view of life (I accept certain things to be of value, and will therefore seek to achieve them).

This last position was that taken by Iris Murdoch, who related moral choice to overall views of reality, such that a particular choice was not made in a vacuum, but related to an understanding of life that had become habitual.

Most importantly, notice that the focus of virtue ethics is set on the nature of the individual who acts. Since virtues are not acquired instantaneously, but developed to the point at which they become habitual, it makes sense to say that a person can seek to develop moral sensitivity, by exercising the virtues in all the choices that he or she makes.

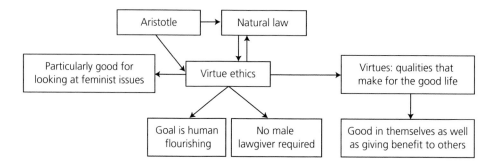

Study guide

By the end of this chapter you should understand how virtue ethics originated in the work of Aristotle, how it relates to natural law, why it is significantly different in approach from Kant and utilitarianism, and why it has appealed to feminist thinkers.

Revision checklist ✓

Can you explain...?

- What is meant by 'human flourishing'.
- Why virtues might depend on circumstances.
- Why virtue ethics generally considers dispositions to act, rather than individual actions.

Do you know...?

- Why virtue ethics is particularly appropriate for feminist issues.
- Why the basis of virtue ethics is similar to that of natural law.

Give arguments for and against...

- The idea that existing ethical theories have been male dominated.

Examples of essay questions

1. Virtue ethics depends on the essence and purpose of human life, and thus on natural law. Discuss.

AO1 requires knowledge of the origins of virtue ethics in Aristotle's idea of the final cause for human beings, and of the 'human flourishing' criterion used in modern virtue ethics.

AO2 needs to argue whether virtue ethics is dependent on such a view of the purpose of human life, or whether the virtues have significance even if no goal for human life is specified.

2. To what extent do the strengths of virtue ethics outweigh its weaknesses as an ethical theory?

AO1 requires knowledge of virtue ethics. Lower level AO1 will tend to give a general summary of virtue ethics, listing some strengths or some weaknesses. Higher level AO1 will focus on both the strengths and weaknesses of virtue ethics and express and structure them in terms of their relevant weightings.

The AO2 must involve some assessment of the weightings of those strengths and weaknesses. Higher level AO2 will make clear the justification for the relative weightings and draw a conclusion that follows from the argument.

Further questions

1 Virtue ethics has no future as an ethical theory. Discuss.

2 There is nothing distinctive about virtue ethics. Assess this claim.

POSTSCRIPT: WHERE DO WE GO FROM HERE?

This book has been concerned with ethical theory – with the general arguments and principles by which people have sought to establish a rational basis for the assessment of moral issues, and also with the consideration of those things that may be regarded as 'good' and 'right' both in terms of actions themselves and the aims and purposes that motivate them.

Many of the thinkers we have considered here were actively concerned to comment on and shape the society of their day. Marx was not strictly accurate when he said that earlier philosophers had sought to understand the world whereas he wanted to change it. There were others – Bentham, for example – who wrote out of their personal involvement in political and social issues. It is equally the case that ethical theory is of limited interest unless it can be seen to be of relevance to practical moral issues. The proof of ethical theory is therefore to be found in applied ethics.

In terms of the academic debate, applied ethics had rather fallen into abeyance during the middle years of the twentieth century, due to the impact of linguistic philosophy and its questions about the nature of language and the validity of moral statements. From the 1930s through until the early 1960s, ethics was dominated by meta-ethical questions. In other words, philosophers were more concerned to ask if moral statements were possible, and how they might be shown to be true or false, than to ask if this or that action was inherently right or wrong. Indeed, A. J. Ayer (in 'The Analysis of Moral Judgements' in *Philosophical Essays*, 1959) thought that people should not look to philosophers for guidance about matters of right and wrong.

Within a decade or so, all that was to change. Influenced perhaps by the radical political and social attitudes of the 1960s, the traumas of the Vietnam War vividly brought to life day by day on television screens, the peace movements, the development of alternative lifestyles and an awareness of the human threat to the environment, there was a demand for new approaches to ethics.

The traditional areas of ethics – sex and relationships, issues of life and death, the nature of law and political rights – were soon to be supplemented by others: feminist ethics, environmental ethics, business ethics. But there was also a growing concern among the professions for ethical guidance. This was seen particularly in the medical and nursing professions, where there was a clear need to define the moral expectations of professional conduct, and also to consider areas of medicine – for example, artificial methods of conception, or euthanasia – where medical and nursing practice sought guidance from clearly defined principles about what would be acceptable to the profession as a whole.

By the beginning of the twenty-first century, the news was dominated by other ethical issues, particularly the moral justification of initiating war, the question of how to understand and counter acts of terrorism, the social and political issues raised by asylum seekers and economic migrants, the effective use of resources in medicine, and the protection of natural resources globally. There was also an overall increase in awareness of the relationship between religious and social attitudes and ethics – with an appreciation of the complexities of living in a multi-ethnic, multi-faith community.

What seems certain – as can be confirmed by looking at almost any daily paper – is that there will continue to be a flourishing interest in applied ethics in one form or another. The pace of social and technological change is so rapid that some professionals feel that they do not have either the opportunity or the expertise to take account of the moral implications of what they do. At the same time, largely influenced by the situation in the USA, the tendency is for those who feel that they have been hurt in any way through the negligence or malpractice of an individual, agency, or state, to have no hesitation in testing their claims in the court and seeking damages. Hence the wariness of professionals who feel themselves to be vulnerable if the ethical implications in what they do, which are potential openings for litigation, have not been properly considered.

There is also a great deal of emotion around in areas of morality, and this is not always harnessed to rational consideration. G. E. Moore may indeed have been right to say that some fundamental concepts, like 'good', are known intuitively, and it may indeed be the case that individuals and groups intuitively sense themselves to have been wronged in some way, or to have right on the side of the cause they fight, but, if that intuition is to lead to positive change (or, indeed, successful litigation), it needs to be backed by carefully reasoned and presented argument. Hence there is a very positive role for applied ethics in the future.

But whereas the practical implications of ethics may have a clear future, the same cannot necessarily be said for ethical theory. Much debate today is based on a combination of theories. Utilitarianism is still prominent in many ethical arguments, contract-based ethics is important in many professional and political situations, and on the personal front there is continued interest in virtue ethics. Very few are prepared to return to the days of Ayer and claim that moral language is meaningless – for when the meaningless becomes a vehicle for litigation it suddenly becomes both real and relevant!

And somewhere in the midst of all this there remains a fundamental quest for 'the good'. Writing in the late 1960s, Iris Murdoch looked at a world in which moral philosophy had become dominated by the effects of linguistic philosophy and also of existentialism. She noted that empiricism, as expounded by Wittgenstein and Russell, had made ethics almost impossible by arguing that moral judgements were not factual. Some assumed that psychology and sociology would supply all the details of personal motivation, rendering conventional moral arguments redundant. Murdoch noted that, in Freudian analysis, objectivity and unselfishness in actions were seen as practically impossible, since the self is motivated by its deepest needs, especially sexual ones.

Others concentrated on the moment of freedom, of self-assertion and of authentic living. But where in all this, Murdoch asked, was there a sense of a complex web of values and virtues? It was almost as if, in surveying the moral landscape, there seemed no place for innocent moral goodness. Although she recognised that an existentialist approach at least offered a philosophy that could be 'lived in', she criticised it as tending towards egocentrism, with the human will taking precedence over the real world outside the self. She saw danger in its attempt to reduce all human virtues to those of freedom and sincerity.

Murdoch also highlighted the fundamental shift in ethics that came as a result of Kant's 'Copernican revolution' (see above, page 93):

> *The centre of this type of post-Kantian moral philosophy is the notion of the will as the creator of value. Values which were previously in some sense inscribed in the heavens and guaranteed by God collapse into the human will. There is no transcendent reality. The idea of the good remains indefinable and empty so that human choice may fill it.*
>
> (*The Sovereignty of Good*, 2001)

Particularly when looking at ethics from a religious perspective, this great hinge in the history of ethics needs to be kept in mind. Looking at Schopenhauer, or Nietzsche, or Heidegger or Sartre, there is the human-centred need to create morality and value, to set a human stamp on the universe that would otherwise be morally neutral and impersonal. That view, right or wrong, is fundamentally at odds with earlier thinking, both religious and secular.

Murdoch therefore returned to the most fundamental of questions: What is a good man like? How can we make ourselves morally better? *Can* we make ourselves morally better? These are the questions the philosopher should try to answer.

In response to the limitations of existing ethical theory, she turned to the Platonic idea of regarding virtue as something that may be perceived and understood (rather than willed and created). She argued that attending to that perception – in Platonic terms, being aware of what is outside and beyond the shadows on the wall of our cave – can lead to the making of morally good choices when the occasion arises.

In this sense, Murdoch saw an 'objective' basis for morality, as for virtue. She linked this with great works of literature and art in which the vision of the artist presents reality in a way that startles us out of the selfish preoccupations of our habitual way of looking. In all this, she sees the narrow concerns of purpose as inadequate to contain a sense of a good that is transcendent, much as Plato's 'Form of the Good' was seen as transcendent. When she comes to define what she means by 'good' she says this:

> *The Good has nothing to do with purpose, indeed it excludes the idea of purpose. 'All is vanity' is the beginning and end of ethics. The only genuine way to be good is to be good 'for nothing' in the midst of the scene where every 'natural' thing, including one's own mind, is subject to chance, that is, to necessity. That 'for nothing' is indeed the experienced correlate of the invisibility or non-representable blankness of the idea of Good itself.*
>
> *(The Sovereignty of Good)*

In other words, she is saying that, if you try to explain 'good' in terms of something else – some ideal future, or universal happiness, for example – then you should be aware that ultimately all such things will turn to dust. Nothing in this world is permanent or ultimate.

But that does not stop us from having a sense that there are some things and actions that are simply 'good', even if we cannot define what we mean by that word, and while this sense of the 'good' remains, there will be a future for ethics.

GLOSSARY

a posteriori used of an argument that depends on sense experience

a priori used of a thought, or moral argument, that arises prior to, or is not based on, a consideration of evidence in the form of sense experience

absolutist used of moral arguments that suggest that it is possible, in theory, to specify moral principles that can be applied universally

act utilitarianism the application of utilitarian theory to individual actions

agapeism moral theory based on the application of love to each situation

altruism the unselfish consideration of others

amoral used for an action that, with respect to the person who performs it, is done without reference to any moral system

applied ethics used for the application of ethical theory to specific issues

ascetic n. one who chooses a life of discipline and austerity; a. used to describe an austere, disciplined life

axiological questions questions about a person's values

Canon Law moral rules set down by the Roman Catholic Church

cardinal virtues prudence, justice, fortitude and temperance; Stoic principles of the moral life, found in Plato and Aristotle and used also by Aquinas

categorical imperative Kant's rational assessment of what is implied by an absolute moral demand (cf. hypothetical imperative)

casuistry the process of applying general moral principles to specific cases (often used critically where such application is done in a rigid manner)

compatibilism the view that a measure of human freedom is compatible with the acceptance of the universal principle of cause and effect

consequentialist ethics any ethical theory based on results (e.g. utilitarianism)

deontological questions questions about a person's rights and duties

descriptive ethics the description of the actual moral choices and values held within a society

determinism philosophical view to the effect that every act is totally conditioned and therefore that agents are not free

dialectic the process of thesis, antithesis and synthesis that Hegel saw as the basic structure of change

doxa Greek term for opinion

emotivism theory that moral statements are in fact expressions of emotion, either approving or disapproving of actions

episteme Greek term for knowledge

equiprobabilism the view that, if two moral judgements are almost equally probable, either can be followed with a good conscience

ethical naturalism the view that goodness exists and can be explained in terms of other features of the world or human life, as in the natural law approach to ethics

ethical non-cognitivism the view that moral statements do not give information, but are merely the expression of the views or wishes of the person who makes them

ethical non-naturalism the view that goodness is not inherent in the world, but is a term we use to describe an object or action

eudaimonia Greek term for happiness

existentialism the general term for the philosophical consideration of an individual's personal sense of meaning and existence, and the overall view of life stemming from such consideration

final cause the final aim or purpose of something

Form a universal reality, in which individual things share (in Plato)

Geworfenheit (Heidegger) 'thrown-ness': the fact that we are born into a particular set of circumstances

hedonic calculus the process (exemplified by Bentham) of attempting to calculate the benefit or harm caused by an act

hypothetical imperative a command to be obeyed only in order to fulfil some limited purpose, taking the form 'do... if you want to achieve...'.

immoral used of behaviour that goes against an accepted set of moral norms

incompatibilism the view that determinism is true and incompatible with the idea of human freedom

intentionality the view that consciousness is always 'about' something, making sense of and relating to external phenomena

intuitionism the view that 'good' is a simple term and may not be further defined, but known through intuition (associated with, but not used by, G. E. Moore)

libertarianism the view that determinism is false and that people are free to act and therefore responsible for their actions

logical positivism philosophical approach which described as meaningful only those statements which could be verified with reference to sense experience (and therefore concluded that ethical statements were meaningless)

logos Greek term for 'word', used of the Christian view of Christ as the 'word' of God in creation, and used by the Stoics for the fundamental rationality in the universe

maxim the moral principle governing an action

the mean Aristotle's idea that doing right involves a balance between extremes

meta-ethics the study of the nature and function of ethical statements

metaphysical ethics an approach that sought to relate ethical claims to an overall view of the nature of reality (see e.g. Bradley)

moral used of behaviour that conforms to an accepted set of norms

natural law ethical theory based on the idea of a 'final cause' or purpose, which defines the proper use or goal of everything

naturalistic fallacy the error (as argued by Hume, G. E. Moore and others) of trying to derive an 'ought' from an 'is'

non-cognitive describes a statement that conveys no factual information; used of an approach to moral claims that relates them exclusively to the emotions and preferences of people who use them

normative ethics a consideration of the principles that influence moral choice and value, used of discussions of what is right, as opposed to descriptions of moral behaviour

preference utilitarianism utilitarian theory taking into account the maximum satisfaction of the preferences of the individuals concerned

prescriptivism the theory that moral statements recommend (or 'prescribe') a particular course of action

probabilism the view (in Catholic moral teaching) that a sufficient body of authoritative opinion is required in order to establish the solid probability that a judgement is correct

proportionalism the principle (e.g. used by Tillich) that there should be a proportional balance between accepting general rules and following the unique demands of each situation

rationalist ethics used of any ethical theory based on reason

reductionism philosophical approach that seeks to 'reduce' everything to basic empirical events (e.g. thoughts are reduced to electric impulses in the brain)

relativist used of moral arguments that consider issues of right and wrong in the light of their particular social, historical or cultural context

rule utilitarianism utilitarian theory that takes into account the benefits gained by following general rules of conduct

syneidesis Greek term for conscience

teleological (approach to ethics) an approach based on the expected end or purpose (*telos*) of an action

telos Greek term for end or purpose

utilitarianism a consequentialist moral theory based on the 'principle of utility', namely the assessment of what will offer the greatest happiness to the greatest number of people involved

virtue ethics ethical theory based on human qualities to be cultivated and expressed through moral choices

TIMELINE OF PHILOSOPHERS

470–399BCE	Socrates
c.428–347BCE	Plato
384–322BCE	Aristotle
341–270BCE	Epicurus
c.334–262BCE	Zeno
50–130CE	Epictetus
121–180CE	Emperor Marcus Aurelius
1225–1274	Thomas Aquinas
1588–1679	Thomas Hobbes
1632–1677	Spinoza
1632–1704	John Locke
1646–1715	Gottfried Leibniz
1671–1713	Earl of Shaftesbury
1692–1752	Bishop Butler
1694–1746	Francis Hutcheson
1711–1776	David Hume
1712–1778	Jean-Jacques Rousseau
1724–1804	Immanuel Kant
1737–1809	Thomas Paine
1748–1832	Jeremy Bentham
1768–1834	Friedrich Schleiermacher
1770–1831	Georg Hegel
1788–1860	Arthur Schopenhauer
1801–1890	John Henry Newman
1806–1873	J. S. Mill
1813–1855	Søren Kierkegaard

1818–1883	Karl Marx
1838–1900	Henry Sidgwick
1844–1900	Friedrich Nietzsche
1871–1947	H. A. Prichard
1873–1958	G. E. Moore
1877–1971	W. D. Ross
1886–1965	Paul Tillich
1889–1951	Ludwig Wittgenstein
1889–1976	Martin Heidegger
1896–1980	Jean Piaget
1900–1980	Eric Fromm
1905–1980	Jean-Paul Sartre
1905–1991	Joseph Fletcher
1908–1979	C. L. Stevenson
1908–1986	Simone de Beauvoir
1910–1989	A. J. Ayer
1917–1981	John Mackie
1919–1999	Iris Murdoch
1919–2001	Elizabeth Anscombe
1919–2002	R. M. Hare
1919–2002	John Rawls
1927–1987	Lawrence Kohlberg
1929–2003	Bernard Williams
1940–	John Finnis
1946–	Peter Singer

To get maximum benefit from this book, it should be used alongside the titles on applied ethics in the *Access to Philosophy and Religion* series:

Michael Wilcockson, *Issues of Life and Death* (Hodder, 2008)
Michael Wilcockson, *Medical Ethics* (Hodder, 2008)
Michael Wilcockson, *Social Ethics* (Hodder, 2009)

Some other useful books include:

Robert Adams, in *Utilitarianism and its Critics* (Macmillan, 1990)
Ray Billington, *Living Philosophy: An Introduction to Moral Thought* (3rd edition) (Routledge, 2003)
Simon Blackburn, *Being Good: An Introduction to Ethics* (OUP, 2001)
T. L. Carson and P. K. Moser (eds), *Morality and the Good Life* (OUP USA, 1997)
Edward Craig (ed.), *The Routledge Encyclopedia of Philosophy* (Routledge, 2000)
R. Crisp and M. Slote (eds), *Virtue Ethics* (OUP, 1997)
Jonathan Glover (ed.), *Utilitarianism and its Critics* (Macmillan USA, 1990)
Jean Holme and John Bowker (eds), *Making Moral Decisions* (Cassell, 1994)
Ted Honderich, *How Free are You?* (OUP, 2002)
Ted Honderich (ed.), *The Oxford Companion to Philosophy* (OUP, 1995)
Alasdair MacIntyre, *A Short History of Ethics* (2nd edition) (Routledge, 2002)
J. L. Mackie, *Ethics: Inventing Right and Wrong* (Penguin, 1977)
Iris Murdoch, *Metaphysics as a Guide to Morals* (OUP, 1994)
Iris Murdoch, *The Sovereignty of Good* (Routledge Classics, 2001)
L. P. Pojman, *Ethics: Discovering Right and Wrong* (Wadsworth, 2001)
James Rachels, *The Elements of Moral Philosophy* (2nd edition) (McGraw-Hill, 1995)
Peter Singer (ed.), *A Companion to Ethics* (Blackwell, 1991)
J. P. Sterba (ed.), *Ethics: The Big Questions* (Blackwell, 1998)
Nigel Warburton, *Philosophy: The Classics* (3rd edition) (Routledge, 2006)
Mary Warnock, *An Intelligent Person's Guide to Ethics* (Duckworth, 1998)

A guide to other books suitable for students, along with information about blogs, magazines and websites for those studying ethics, may be found at the **Philosophy and Ethics** resource site, at: www.philosophyandethics.com.

On-line resources for this book and others in the series

New books and websites are appearing all the time.
Keep up-to-date and share your own suggestions
with other students and teachers.

For suggestions for further reading, comments from the authors
of the *Access to Religion and Philosophy* series and further advice for students and teachers,
log on to the *Access to Religion and Philosophy*
website at:

www.philosophyandethics.com/access.htm

INDEX